# ANCIENT INDIANS

# ANCIENT INDIANS

## The First Americans

**Roy A. Gallant**

ENSLOW PUBLISHERS, INC.

Bloy St. & Ramsey Ave.    P.O. Box 38
Box 777    Aldershot
Hillside, N.J. 07205    Hants GU12 6BP
U.S.A.    U.K.

**Library of Congress Cataloging-in-Publication Data**

Gallant, Roy A.
    Ancient Indians.

    Summary: Describes how the first Indians arrived
from Asia and how their society developed in different
parts of North America.
    1. Indians of North America--History--Juvenile
literature. 2. Indians of North America--Antiquities--
Juvenile literature. [1. Indians of North America--
History. 2. Indians of North America--Antiquities]
I. Title.
E77.4.G35          1989          970.01          87-36526
ISBN 0-89490-187-7

Printed in the United States of America

10 9 8 7 6 5 4 3 2 1

**Illustration Credits:**
Stephen Bicknell: p. 33; Roy A. Gallant: p. 71; Metropolitan Museum of
Art, gift of George D. Pratt, 1933: p. 75; National Geographic Society,
Richard H. Stewart Photo, c. 1939: p. 65; National Park Service: p. 19;
National Park Service, George A. Grant Photo: pp. 83, 84, 85, 97; Na-
tional Park Service, Fred Mang Photo: p. 48; National Park Service,
Fred Mang Jr. Photo: p. 82; Science Photo/Graphics: pp. 15, 18, 24, 26,
35, 41, 46, 53, 67, 69, 88, 89, 90; University of Colorado Museum, Joe
Ben Wheat Photo: p. 16.

FOR MAURICE AND ANTOINETTE

# Acknowledgments

The author wishes to thank Dr. Richard Michael Gramly, of the Buffalo Museum of Science, for reviewing the manuscript of this book for technical accuracy and for his statement in the Foreword. My thanks also to Dr. Robson Bonnichsen, Director of the Center for the Study of Early Man, the University of Maine at Orono, for reading selected passages for accuracy and for providing photographs demonstrating the technique of fashioning projectile points from chert using only deer antler bone. My thanks also to Jane Livingston, also of the Center for the Study of Early Man, for so efficiently arranging—at the last minute—for photographs and caption material explaining the process of flintknapping. The assistance of Rick Lewis of the National Park Service, U.S. Department of the Interior, in locating photographs of American Indian sites and artifacts, was invaluable. My thanks also to Jeanine L. Dickey for her help with photo research, and finally, my thanks to Macmillan Publishing Company for permission to adapt, for inclusion in the present book, the passage describing radiocarbon dating from my book *Earth's Changing Climate,* © 1979 by Roy A. Gallant.

# Contents

# Preface

When we try to explain the peopling of North and South America we must ask five questions: When? Where? How? By whom? And, why did people come here anyway?

Scholars have written many papers on this large topic but no one has answered all five questions to my satisfaction. All of the known genetic, linguistic, and archaeological evidence suggest that the ancestors of the American Indians came from Asia. That is pretty well established, or so it seems. Also, most of us engaged in sorting out the pieces of this peopling puzzle agree that the earliest immigrants of what is now the United States came across a bridge of land that has linked present day Alaska with Siberia during times of lowered sea level off and on over the past tens of thousands of years. Or, alternatively, the immigrants may have paddled their way along the Pacific Rim in small boats. But no one has yet provided a convincing motive for why people came here in the first place, if, indeed, they had a motive to come here!

*When* human populations first began the long trek from Asia to the Americas is hotly debated among archaeologists. Some say it began not much earlier than about 12,000 years ago. Others say it happened much earlier. I happen to be among those who favor a "much earlier" date. For evidence we have the following: flaked mammoth bone dated greater than 30,000 years old from sites in the Old Crow Basin of the northern Yukon Territory; altered bones from El Cedral, northern Mexico more than 33,000 years old, and a long sequence of simple pebble and flake tools from Toca do Boqueirão da Pedra Furada, Brazil, extending back to more than 40,000 years ago.

But were there people here in the Americas even earlier? Some scholars think that small populations could have been here as early as 250,000 years ago, but convincing evidence has yet to be turned up. As you will find as you read this book, there are "early arrivalist" theories, "middle arrivalist" theories, and "late arrivalist" theories. No matter what our respective view happens to be as archaeologists, those of us involved in taking some of the mystery out of the peopling of the Americas all agree that we have much more to do to come up with an acceptable explanation for the colonization of the Americas. Dr. Gramly, who wrote the foreword to this book, is one of the many scholars digging out the facts. So are we at the Center for the Study of Early Man at the University of Maine. It is important that all of us keep an open mind to any new evidence that may shed light on the earliest cultural heritage of the Americas.

Dr. Robson Bonnichsen
Director
Center for the Study of Early Man
University of Maine, at Orono

# Foreword

When I was ten years old, I discovered my first Indian arrowhead and knew that I wanted to become an archaeologist. Popularly written books like Ceram's *Gods, Graves and Scholars* and Robbins's *Hidden America* fueled my growing interest in archaeology. For years I believed that digging was the principal stuff of archaeology, but gradually it became clear to me that archaeologists work on many levels.

There are field-workers who discover and map new archaeological sites. Others spend most of their time excavating and gathering new evidence. Afterward in the laboratory there are teams of archaeologists who catalog artifacts and perform special tests, such as radiocarbon dating, seed and bone identifications, and analysis of plant pollen. All this labor by many specialists comes to fruit when archaeologists who are skilled writers and speechmakers present their findings to audiences of scientists. But even then the job is not finished.

Most archaeologists believe that the public must be informed about new discoveries and gains in knowledge, for public support makes archaeology and other sciences flourish. Newspaper accounts and television broadcasts cannot provide the full story. Out of necessity some archaeologists have authored popular publications. More often they rely upon skilled professional writers to tell their story.

Roy A. Gallant is one of these spokesman for archaeology, and his service is valuable, indeed. In this book about Paleo-Indians and their successors he summarizes hard-won evidence that has been accumulating for nearly sixty years.

Paleo-Indians are a people very close to my heart. I have been following their footsteps and excavating their encampments since 1966 when I discovered my first fluted point on a rocky ridge high above the Hudson River south of Albany, New York.

11

Paleo-Indians have a unique place in human prehistory. They were colonizers of a New World. These supremely efficient hunters, heir to millions of years of cultural evolution, stepped out into unexplored lands teeming with animals. The highly developed, complex civilizations that the Spanish conquistadores met when they went ashore in Mexico are proof that Paleo-Indians successfully met all the challenges that lay before them.

Dr. Richard Michael Gramly
Curator of Anthropology
Buffalo Museum of Science
Buffalo, N.Y.

# 1
# *Bison Kill*

## A Hunt-Chief's Tale

If they had been able to write it all down about 10,000 years ago, they might have left a record something like this:

> The trap was ready by noon. Since midmorning many of our band of about eighty people had been tramping down the soft snow to form a wide solid path to the steep slope of the old riverbed. At this place the riverbed formed a natural bowl. It made a good trap, one large enough to hold bison, many bison. The snow trampers were young men, strong and quick at throwing the spears we fashion of wooden rods tipped with sharp stone blades.
>
> While our hunters readied the trap, others of our people kept track of a nearby herd of bison pawing away the snow to eat the grass beneath. The herd was a winter group of females with their young. All the bull bison had left the herd in the autumn to form all-male groups, as is the custom of these beasts. Those of our people watching the herd were our women, older children, and old men who no longer had the strength and swiftness of limb to

kill a bison. They were waiting for a sign from me, the hunt-chief, that the trap was ready. After praying to the spirits of the animals I waved a signal to those watching the herd. They began shouting and waving hides to stampede the herd toward the trap. Earlier we had made a fence of sticks and brush to form a funnel leading to the hard-packed and now slippery entrance to the trap.

We watched as the bison began moving toward us, first at a trot and then at a gallop as the shouting and waving of hides worked the animals into a frenzy. Guided by our fence and driven from behind, the bison neared our trap. By the time they reached the entrance they were at full gallop and threw so much snow in the air that they took the appearance of a large cloud rushing toward us. On reaching the packed and slippery entrance many lost their footing and tumbled down the steep slope and into the deep soft snow at the bottom, as was our plan. Those that managed to keep their footing soon were tripped up by those that had fallen. They, too, became helpless and were easy targets for our hunters who hurled their spears with spear-thrower sticks. Some of the animals were killed instantly, others were mortally wounded. All, wounded or not, soon were helpless in the deep snow and became heaped one on top of another as still more tumbled down the slope. Very soon our trap had claimed more than fifty animals. When they had stopped thrashing about I directed the hunters to slide down among the animals and quickly put them to death to prevent needless suffering.

The hunt had been successful and our group was in high spirits. We had had little to eat for many days past but would not be hungry again this winter. Our lives depend on the bison. They provide us with food. With their skins we make foot coverings and warm clothing and robes to protect us from frostbite. With their bones we fashion spear points and other tools. Little of a slaughtered animal is wasted. This small herd will keep us alive and warm for several moons.

14

## Who Were the Ancient Hunters?

Did such a mass slaughter of bison actually take place some 10,000 years ago? Without doubt, say anthropologists, scientists who study the customs and ways of people living today and who lived long ago. Among such scientists is Dennis Stanford of the Smithsonian Institution in Washington, D.C. In June 1973, Stanford looked at a site near Wray, Colorado, discovered earlier by rancher Robert B. Jones, Jr. "There are bones all over the place!" Stanford was informed by another scientist who had visited Jones. And there were projectile points for spear tips, too. In all, there were some 41,000 pieces of bison bones at the site. There also were more than 300 stone and bone projectile points and several flint knives and choppers, both tools used to cut up slaughtered animals.

The bone pile studied by Stanford actually marked the second stage of a huge bison kill. The bones had been arranged in groups—leg bones piled here, ribs in other piles, skulls in another, and so on. This arrangement suggested that the hunt and butchering that followed had been well organized. Another famous bison-kill took place at the Olsen-Chubbuck site in southeastern Colorado about 8,500 years ago. Archaeologists found about 200 bison skeletons forming

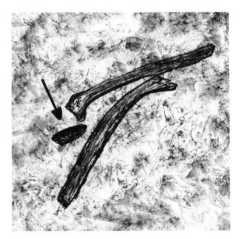

The first proof that ancient Indians were in America just after the last Ice Age, more than 10,000 years ago, came from a stone projectile point *(see arrow)* found between two fossil ribs of an extinct bison. The find was made in New Mexico in 1927.

15

a pile about 12 feet (4 m) wide and 7 feet (2 m) deep. Because the animals at the bottom of the heap were hard to reach right after the bison were killed, many of their skeletons were undisturbed. Most of the remaining animals had been skillfully butchered and their bones separated and piled in an orderly way as at the Wray site.

Who were these early Americans who lived about 10,000 years ago and were such highly skilled hunters? Where did they come from? Did their ancestors also live in the American West even longer ago—50,000 years ago? 100,000 years ago? These questions are at the heart of one of the most exciting of today's science mysteries: Who were the first Americans?

Mass killings of bison by Paleo-Indians have been unearthed at sites such as Olsen-Chubbuck in Colorado. Careful excavation by archaeologists reveals many details of such events.

# 2

## A Land of Ice

To understand something of the lives of the early Americans who roamed what is now the American West some 10,000 and more years ago, we must turn back the geologic clock to about 18,000 years ago and ask what North America was like then.

### Ages of Ice

That time marked the peak of the last glacial period. In our planet's long history of some 4.6 billion years, many ages of ice have come and gone. And many more surely are to follow. About 30 percent of the earth's total land surface was covered with ice during the last glacial period—including parts of both the Northern and Southern Hemispheres. In northern Labrador and central Norway, for example, the ice probably first formed into glaciers in the mountain regions. These so-called mountain glaciers then grew into sprawling ice sheets that gradually crept southward and covered the land with several thousand feet of ice. While the average thickness of ice was about 4 thousand feet (1,200m), or nearly a mile, it probably

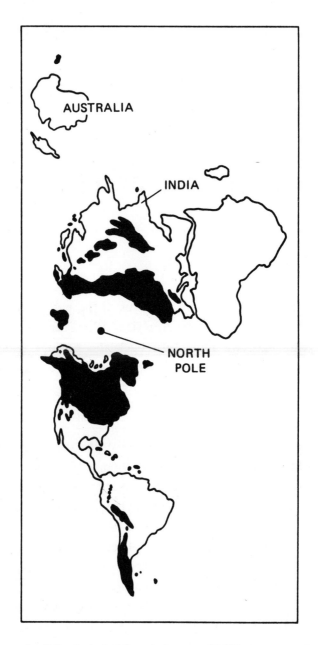

At the peak of the last glacial period, some 18,000 years ago, ice *(dark regions in the diagram)* covered about 30 percent of earth's land surface.

was more than twice that deep over all of Canada and most of the United States as far south as the Ohio and Missouri rivers. The Greenland and Antarctic ice caps today are reminders of how parts of North America looked then. The Greenland ice cap is 2 miles (3 km) deep today. That is enough ice to cover the earth's entire surface to a depth of nearly 20 feet (6 m).

Glacial periods seem to come and go in cycles. Over the past 700,000 years, for example, there have been seven known glacial periods. Each has been separated from the next by a period of warming called an interglacial period. Those of us now living in the Northern Hemisphere may be enjoying one such warm interglacial period. Scientists who study the

The Ruth Glacier is an example of a mountain glacier and a reminder of what it was like during the last glacial period. This glacier can be seen today in Mount McKinley National Park, Alaska.

19

earth's changing climate tell us that about 13,000 years ago there was a warming period and the great ice began to retreat. As it did, grasslands once again took hold and large herds of grazing animals occupied the warming land right up to the edge of the ice. Wherever there were grazing animals there were predators, such as large cats and wolves, who fed on them. And where there was game, usually there were human predators.

By the end of the last glacial period about 10,000 years ago, North America was the home of a wide variety of species of animals, many now extinct. Fossils from different parts of North America are evidence that beasts, large and small, roamed the land. Among the giants were mammoths, elephantlike animals that stood 13 feet (4 m) high at the shoulders and waved massive curving tusks just as long. They may have used their tusks as snowplows to uncover vegetation on which they fed. The woolly mammoth, which stood 9 feet (3 m) high and was adapted to life on the cold northern plains, was a model of insulation. It had a 3-inch (8-cm)-deep layer of fat covered by thick skin which in turn was covered by an undercoat of wool topped by long, shaggy hair.

## Mastodons and Saber-toothed Cats

The giant mastodons, ancestors of today's Indian and African elephants, also were awesome beasts that roamed the northeastern United States in great numbers. More than 100 mastodon skeletons have been found in New York State. The remains of mastodons, and of giant saber-toothed cats, also have been found in the famous La Brea Tar Pits in Los Angeles, California. The giant beavers, as large as a black bear and with teeth the size of an ax blade, could probably gnaw their way through a tree in minutes. The giant short-faced bears of the period were larger and swifter runners than today's grizzly bears. And there were lions larger than today's lions, and long-horned bison with a six-foot span of horns. There also were horses, camels, yaks, musk-oxen, moose, caribou, and woolly rhinoceroses. Enormous ground sloths the size of elephants reared up on their hind legs to eat leaves and tender shoots growing two stories above the ground. South America also had its giants, among them rats the size of a calf and meat-eating birds that stood 8 feet (2 m) high.

Why so many giant animals? According to biologists, a cold climate favors the survival of large animals since they lose body heat at a slower rate than do smaller animals. Some of these animals, such as ground sloths and armadillos, came northward into the southern United States from South America. Others, such as saber-toothed cats, mammoths, antelopes, and musk-oxen, crossed over a broad bridge of land then exposed and linking Alaska with Asia. As the drawing on page 26 shows, most of what is now Alaska had only scattered patches of glacial ice.

During a glacial period much of the earth's ocean water is locked up as ice. The water evaporates, falls as snow, and then the snow is packed into ice. The result is a much lowered sea level. Today huge amounts of water are locked up in the Greenland and Antarctic ice caps. There is so much that if all that ice suddenly melted, enough water would be added to the oceans to raise the sea level by about 300 feet (90 m). Hundreds of coastal cities around the world, including New York, Hong Kong, and Tokyo, for example, would be underwater.

Some 10,000 years ago near the close of the last glacial period, world sea level was perhaps 325 feet (98 m) lower than it is today and exposed the broad flat floors of the Bering and Chukchi seas between Alaska and Siberia. The sprawling land bridge was about 1,000 miles (1,600 km) wide and has been named Beringia, after the Bering Strait. During the many glacial periods over the past several hundred thousand years, Beringia has surfaced from time to time only to be swallowed up again by glacier meltwater. But each time it surfaced it remained high and dry for a thousand years or more, permitting the movement of animals from Siberia to North America and in the opposite direction. For instance, horses and camels, which evolved in North America, migrated westward across Beringia into Asia while moose and caribou, which were natives of Asia, migrated eastward into North America along with other species.

Another land feature that is important, but not essential, in our account of the arrival of the first Americans was an ice-free corridor leading from Alaska southward between the massive ice sheets to warmer regions. Some say that such a corridor opened up from time to time during brief warming periods. Others doubt that such a corridor ever served as a highway for wandering bands of people. If it did, they argue, then where is the evidence that people once passed that way? The corridor supposedly ran southward along the eastern slopes of the Rockies, separating the two superglaciers known as the Cordilleran and Laurentide glaciers.

With that as our setting some 13,000 or more years ago, we may now ask who the first human beings were to arrive on that scene, where they came from, and why they came.

# 3
# *Overland From Asia?*

So far as we can tell, the first human beings to set foot in America came from Asia and they came aimlessly, in pursuit of big game. They trod some 55 miles (88 km) across a broad landmass serving as a "bridge" linking Siberia to Alaska before the close of the last ice age, about 11,000 years ago. Some archaeologists think that the first Paleo-Indians came much earlier—from 14,000 to 50,000 years ago, or maybe 100,000 years ago. (Paleo- is from the Greek word *palaios* and means "ancient.") Archaeologists use the term Paleo-Indian to describe those early Americans whose bone or stone tools, or other artifacts, have been found along with the extinct giant animals of the last ice age.

## Across the Beringian Land Bridge
As glacial periods have gripped North America from time to time and the ocean level has lowered, the Siberian land bridge has come and gone. It existed still earlier, from about 25,000 to 14,000 years ago, for example. It also existed briefly before 35,000 years ago. Because this broad northern region receives

23

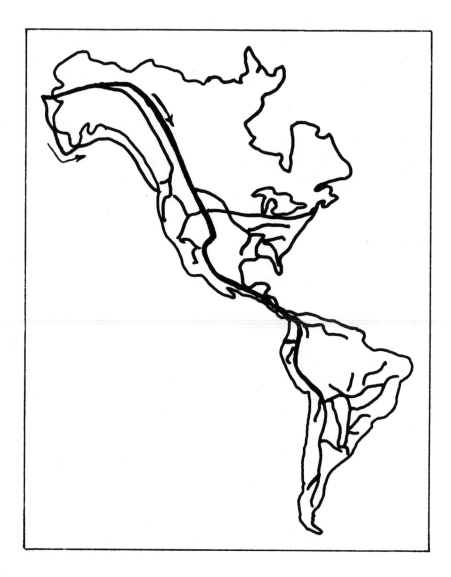

Of the many possible migration routes that the Paleo-Indians and their descendants could have taken to populate North and South America, several are shown here, as suggested by Carl Sauer.

relatively little moisture, the land bridge along with sprawling areas of Alaska and the Northern Yukon were grasslands that escaped the ice so plentiful elsewhere, conditions similar to ice-covered parts of northern Scandinavia today. It was an Arctic Eden with big game aplenty to support scattered small populations of Paleo-Indians. So far, archaeologists have studied about a dozen Paleo-Indian sites in Alaska. They have found bone tools and other remains that show that the owners lived there from about 7,400 to more than 10,000 years ago.

We must not suppose that these first Americans had any destination in mind as over the decades and centuries they moved gradually southward. They simply followed the animals as a source of food and along the way southward found that the climate became less harsh. Where the herds were large and berries and other wild foods plentiful, the Paleo-Indians lingered. Sometimes their stops lasted months, other times years or a lifetime. They stopped where the land was good to them and had no idea of what lay around the next bend. They were hunters and food gatherers. Planned farming was unknown to these people. If a group moved on by only a mile, (1.6 km) or so a year, in one generation it would move about 20 miles (32 km). In a hundred years, the original group's offspring would have moved about 2,000 miles (3,200 km).

But surely there were explorers among these first Americans. It is human nature to be curious, to want to know what lies beyond that distant mountain or around the bend of that broad river. Perhaps small bands of such inquisitive and daring individuals set out in search of a better life than the one they had and moved southward hundreds of miles in a lifetime. Possibly it was one or more such hardy groups who are known to have lived in New Mexico 11,600 years ago. We can imagine them moving southward from Alaska along the eastern edge of the Rockies between the two superglaciers and

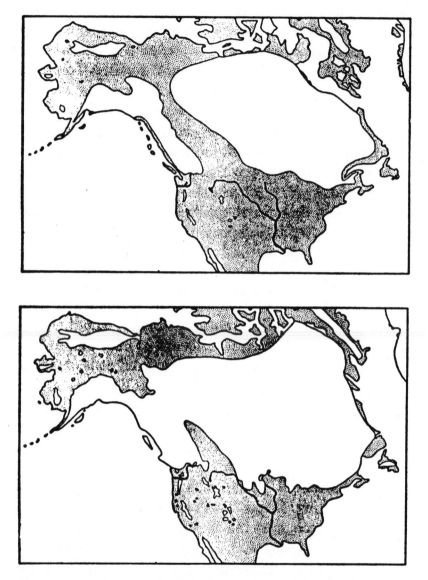

The main migration route the Paleo-Indians followed from north to south probably was along an ice-free corridor which had opened up by at least 10,000 years ago (top). About 15,000 years ago, after the peak of the last glacial period, the corridor may have just begun to open from the south (bottom).

out onto the ice-free Great Plains, drawn southward by an ever warming climate. If they did, in fact, pass that way, no trace of them has yet been found.

## Was a Coastal Route Possible?

Some scientists who study Paleo-Indian cultures think that southward routes might have been along the Pacific coast. One such scientist is Knut Fladmark, an archaeologist at Simon Fraser University in British Columbia, Canada. One reason they give is that the Beringian land bridge and the ice-free corridor between the Laurentide and Cordilleran super-glaciers seem unlikely to have existed at the same time and so permitting a steady flow of people southward. The land bridge, they point out, would be exposed only during a cold period when the sea level is low. But a warm period would be needed for an opening of an ice-free corridor. Hence an argument for some groups moving southward along the coast at a time when the corridor was closed.

Why does Fladmark think that a coastal route was possible? For thousands of years people lived along the coast of northeast Asia and managed a living from the sea. It would be natural, he reasons, for such coastal groups to favor a coastal route southward instead of an inland route. Food along a coast is easy to come by for people who have learned to depend on the sea for their livelihood.

Still other students of Paleo-Indian cultures think that some groups could have sailed from Asia eastward across the Pacific Ocean. A likely route would have been along northern Japan, the Kurile Islands, the Kamchatka Peninsula, and the Aleutian Islands to Alaska. Evidence for early people skilled in ocean travel was discovered in Australia in 1968. Australia is an island continent and could be reached by humans only by boat. Archaeological digs there have turned up evidence that people were living in Australia at least 40,000 years ago, and probably much earlier. Is it possible, then, that people that long ago also could have crossed the vast expanse of the Pacific Ocean, sailing from southeast Asia to South America? Although some scholars feel that such long ocean voyages were technically possible, it is hard to imagine a group setting sail eastward into the Pacific Ocean not knowing if they ever would find land. One reason for many scholars favoring the Beringia land route is that Beringia was a continuous landmass.

## Evidence for an Asian Origin

There was plenty of time for groups to have arrived in the Americas by both land and sea. In China between the latitude of northern Florida and New York there are at least eight known sites more than 100,000 years old. Farther north at a latitude between that of New York and southern Alaska are about ten sites from 40,000 to 100,000 years old and another forty or so sites 11,000 to 40,000 years old. Add to those about a dozen sites in Japan 18,000 to 100,000 years old.

How do we know that the first Americans came from Asia at all? What evidence have archaeologists and anthropologists come up with? First, the earliest human beings did not evolve in America so the Paleo-Indians must have come from a place other than America. There is a strong likeness in appearance of American Indians living today and northern Asians—coppery skin, dark eyes, wide cheekbones, and straight black hair. Also, northern Asians living during the last ice age and living today have teeth that are very much alike and different in a minor but important way from the teeth of other people. Among the scientists who have studied the tooth similarities of northern Asians and American Indians is Christy G. Turner II of Arizona State University. The forward biting teeth of both groups have a scooped-out appearance called "shoveling." Turner says that tooth shoveling evolved about 40,000 years ago.

So far in our account of America's first settlers, we know that they arrived here at least 11,000 years ago, that they came from northeastern Asia, and that their most likely route was across the Beringian land bridge. We further know that over the following years they pushed ever southward until groups reached the southern tip of South America. They also swiftly populated the broad expanse of North America from Florida to Maine. The first such groups we will see through the eyes of scientific sleuths are known as the Clovis people, named after their campsites discovered in Clovis, New Mexico.

# 4

## *The Clovis People*

In 1932 paleontologists digging at a site called Blackwater Draw near the town of Clovis, New Mexico, and at a second site at Dent near Denver, Colorado, uncovered stone spear points unlike any others in the world. At the time nothing was known about these projectile points or about the people who made them. Some diggers even referred to the points as "arrowheads," although they were much too large to have been the tip of an arrow. So far as we know, the bow and arrow were not to be invented for thousands of years after the first Clovis point was fashioned by highly skilled craftsmen.

When archaeologists and paleontologists dig at a site they carefully pick and brush away the rock in which they find an artifact, bone, or other remains. They are especially careful to record the exact position in which each bone and artifact was found. To do so, they draw maps of their digging site and take photographs as the dig proceeds. You can see the importance of keeping such a detailed record of an archaeological dig in the following account of the first important find of a Paleo-Indian site.

## Crowfoot Ranch's Remarkable "Cow"

The year was 1908, the place a few miles outside Folsom, New Mexico, and the person a rock-hound cowboy named George McJunkin. He was inspecting fence posts on the Crowfoot Ranch and came across some large bones sticking out of the walls of a ditch about 10 feet (3 m) below the surface. The bones were too big to be those of a cow and too deep to have been buried by a man. His interest in rock collecting and fossils caused him to stop and study the bones. Later he described his find to the local blacksmith, Carl Schwachheim, who was also interested in fossils. And there the matter rested until 1922.

In that year Schwachheim organized a small digging party and drove over the bumpy roads to the Crowfoot Ranch site. And there were the bones, in even greater abundance than McJunkin had reported. Over the years heavy rains had gulleyed the cut more and had further exposed the archaeological treasure. Eagerly, the group dug out "nearly a sack full," brought them back to town, and tried to identify them. But they were not like bones they had ever seen before.

Eventually Schwachheim wrote to the Colorado Museum of Natural History in Denver and described the find. The museum's director, Jesse D. Figgins, had a good nose for a bone find and told Schwachheim that he would pay a visit to the site. By that time it was 1926. It is important to mention here that earlier Figgins had learned of a similar site in Texas where unusually large bones, and three large projectile points, had been found. But the bones along with the projectile points had been carelessly dug up and their positions in relation to each other not recorded. Figgins jumped at the chance to examine what appeared to be an undisturbed site at the Crowfoot Ranch and directed his son to begin excavation in 1926. Figgins himself was off on a dig in Texas. Sure

Modern-day craftsmen have relearned the technique of making projectile points for spears as they were made by Paleo-Indians 10,000 years ago. Robson Bonnichsen, Director of the Center for the Study of Early Man, the University of Maine, demonstrates the art of pressure flaking a projectile point by using deer antler bone to work a piece of chert.

enough, Figgins, Jr., found bison bones galore, bones that did not match the bones of living bison. In one instance he uncovered broken pieces of a projectile point lying beside a bison's backbone. In August of the next year another projectile point was uncovered, this one almost touching the rib of a bison.

Figgins, Sr., fired off telegrams to the major museums of the United States inviting their scientists to come and see for themselves. The experts came and looked and shared Figgins's excitement. Still more priceless finds were soon to be made at the site—twenty-three bison skeletons associated with nineteen projectile points. Here was the first major Paleo-Indian archaeological find ever made and proof that an extinct animal had been killed by human beings using a projectile point fashioned long ago. But how long ago? Later, scientific dating methods showed that the bison bones were at least 10,000 years old, which meant that the projectile points themselves and the people who made them also were at least 10,000 years old.

## Clovis Versus Folsom Points

It turned out that the 1927 Folsom find and the 1932 Dent and Blackwater Draw finds were quite different. The Clovis projectile points unearthed at the latter two sites were larger and older than the Folsom points found at the Crowfoot Ranch. Large and rugged, the Clovis points are described as fluted and bifacial. A bifacial point is one that has been chipped by striking flakes from both sides. When the 3- to 4-inch (7.6- to 10.2-cm)-long point was all but finished, the toolmaker struck final hollows at each side of the base of the point to make flutes. These enabled the end of a long spear or shorter stick to be fitted to the base of the projectile point, tied to the shaft by thong, and probably held in place with some kind of natural glue such as blood, which works very well.

Clovis points are beautifully made of glasslike or fine-grained stone such as obsidian or chert. It was the fluted nature of the points that made them different from any other projectile points in the world, and that made them such an excellent weapon. One archaeologist who needed surgery a few years ago equipped his doctor with cutting blades made of obsidian. The surgeon said that the blades were sharper than his steel scalpels.

Folsom points were smaller and more elegant. Instead of striking the point to chip off flakes, people of the Folsom culture pressure-flaked their points. This meant pressing a

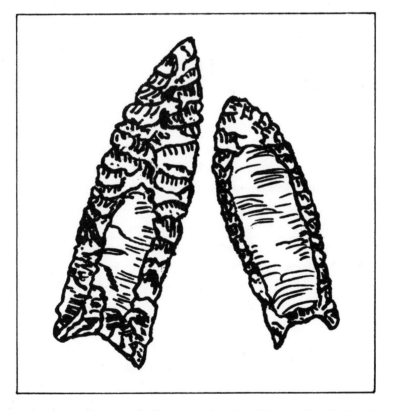

A Clovis projectile point (left) compared with a Folsom point. Both points are flaked on both sides, which makes them "bifacial." Both points have hollows, which permitted them to be fitted to the end of a shaft.

tool hard enough at a spot near the point's edge to chip off a small flake. By working around the edge of the point in this way, an elegant and razor-sharp cutting blade can be made. The Folsom people improved on the Clovis point by refining it. Made of the same materials as Clovis points, also fluted and bifacial, Folsom points were smaller, more streamlined, and the fluting was improved by being extended nearly the entire length of the point on both faces. Because of the thinness and two-sided flutes of the Folsom points, about a third of the points were broken while being chipped. The efficiency of these delicate points outweighed the difficulty in making them.

Breakthroughs in technology of this nature rarely are the result of accident or pure invention. More likely the stoneworker as a child watched his father or some other stoneworker fashion projectile points and later copied what he saw, perhaps improving on it in some small way either by accident or by design. Or groups met and traded tools or weapons, in which case the superior tools would be copied. In some such way primitive tools sometimes evolved into excellence from one generation to the next, or within a single generation.

The difference between the Clovis and Folsom points became even more significant when archaeologists working at the Blackwater Draw site found not one but two layers of bones and artifacts. This was evidence that two different cultures had lived and hunted in the area at different times. The bottom Clovis layer had to be the older of the two. Just such layering often has been the case at archaeological digs. Excavators have discovered enormous mounds built up over the centuries by different cultures establishing a city on top of a site where others had built and lived earlier. And so the mound grew ever higher.

The Clovis culture included many tools. Among them was a spear throwing stick, called an atlatl, used earlier by Cro-Magnon men in France. Eskimos used it for seal and polar bear hunting and to this day it is used by Australian aborigines and called the woomera. They also used stone scrapers for working animal hides, hammers, and made fine needles of bone for sewing hides to make boots and clothing.

In April 1988 archaeologists digging in an apple orchard near Wenatchee, Washington uncovered what may be the first intact group of Clovis artifacts. "This is a startling discovery," said Mike Gramley, one of the archaeologists on the dig, and author of the Foreword of this book. "We've finally found Clovis material in its original position," he added, "and if the site is carefully excavated, it will enable us to address important questions about these people." The find turned out to be the largest group of Clovis points ever discovered and included stone scrapers and fleshers and antler bone tools.

Craftsmen of the Clovis culture were inventive and expert workers in stone and bone. If it was not these people themselves who soon inhabited nearly every corner of North and South America, then it was people who came in contact with them and copied their technology. For Clovis points were to appear by the thousands across North America.

# 5
# *How the Clovis Culture Spread*

Radiocarbon dating of Clovis culture remains show that these inventive people had lived at the Blackwater Draw and Wenatchee sites between 11,000 and 11,600 years ago. The Folsom remains found in the upper layer of the Blackwater Draw site show that this later culture—probably descendants of the Clovis people—lived there from at least 10,000 to 10,500 years ago.

Clovis technology virtually exploded across North America eastward to Nova Scotia and southward to Virginia. In the west it was soon to reach as far south as Chile in South America. And Clovislike projectile points some 10,700 years old have been found in a site known as Fell's Cave at the southern tip of South America.

This much scientist-sleuths trying to solve the complex puzzle of the Paleo-Indians agree on. But how did the Clovis culture spread across a continent so fast?

### How Old Is a Bone?
When archaeologists dig up fossils of living material, they want to know how old the once-living remains are. One

means of doing this is the carbon-14 method. Because all living matter known to us contains carbon, this chemical element can be used as an atomic clock to date the remains of bone or of charcoal from an ancient campfire, for example. Here is how radiocarbon dating works:

Ordinary carbon is in the form chemists call carbon-12. (The number 12 tells us how many of certain particles called protons are contained in the nucleus of each atom.) A heavier form of carbon called carbon-14 is used in radiocarbon dating. Carbon-14 is continuously being produced in the air out of the chemical element nitrogen-14. This happens when nitrogen-14 is bombarded by energetic particles from space (cosmic rays).

The leaves of all green plants take in carbon-14 from the air, along with carbon-12, as the leaves "breathe" in carbon dioxide day and night. Since almost all animals eat green plants, animals also take in carbon-14.

When a plant or animal dies, it stops taking in carbon. The carbon-14 it has at the time of death then begins to break down. When an old bone, shell, or other piece of once-living matter being dated is analyzed, the scientist compares the number of carbon-14 atoms to the number of carbon-12 atoms. That comparison (ratio) gives an estimate of the age of the once-living bone or shell. The less carbon-14, the older the bone or piece of shell is. The radiocarbon method of dating once-living matter is reliable for remains up to about 100,000 years old.

The radiocarbon method of dating has been useful in dating wood, charcoal, rope, peat, bones, marine shells, and other once-living matter.

In 1980 I had the good fortune to be part of an archaeological dig at the Vail site in the western mountains of Maine near the Canadian border. The archaeologist in charge was Mike Gramly, of the Buffalo Museum of Science. Four months of methodical digging produced 10,000 stone artifacts, including nearly 5,000 tools. In Gramly's words, "the tally at the Vail site was one of the most productive early hunter stations in eastern North America." One day a visiting archaeologist strolling along the shore of Lake Aziscohos where the dig was taking place spied a fluted projectile point lying on the beach as if dropped there that morning. According to Gramly, "the specimen was one of the finest we had found since the onset of excavation in June." The same day Gramly found "a magnificent fluted projectile point, complete in every detail after lying in the sands for 11,000 years."

Anthropologist Mike Gramly on a Paleo-Indian dig at the Vail site, located in the western mountain region of Maine. The site was dated at about 10,000 years old.

If people giving rise to the Clovis culture crossed over from Beringia into the New World some 10,000 to 12,000 years ago, their descendants were living in New Mexico 400 years later, having covered a distance of some 2,500 miles to reach New Mexico. Then in 1,000 years the Clovis culture had spread to the farthest habitable reaches of both North and South America.

According to Paul S. Martin of the University of Arizona, the Paleo-Indian hunters crossing Beringia might have moved southward at the rate of about 10 miles (16 km) a year. If they doubled their numbers every generation, in only 300 years their population could have grown to 300,000 people and they would have reached the Gulf of Mexico and eastern United States. In another 700 years they would have been long established in the remotest outposts at the tip of South America in a cold and bitter land called Tierra del Fuego. If that was the case, then various groups settled in different regions—some in the mountains, others along the coast, and still others in the rugged and hostile far southern latitudes.

**The Environment Shapes Populations**
Over the thousands of years that followed, those different local populations would have adapted to their local environment and developed noticeable individual cultural and physical makeups. A culture is always shaped by the elements of its environment. This fact can be seen today as we study different cultures around the world. For example, Indians who live at 15,000-foot (4,570-m) heights in the Andes of South America are different from populations living at sea level. Over the many centuries of living a mountain life they have developed larger chests, greater lung capacities, more blood, and more gas exchange lung structures (alveoli) than people living at sea level. These physical changes, according to

Marshall T. Newmann, an anthropologist, have enabled the Indians to live comfortably in an atmosphere with only one-half the pressure at sea level. The short fingers of Eskimos are another example of a population adaptation, in this case one that reduces heat loss in a cold climate. The dark skin of tropical climate people in an adaptation that protects skin damage by ultraviolet radiation, which is more intense in equatorial regions than at higher latitudes.

When the British naturalist Charles Darwin visited the harsh land of Tierra del Fuego in 1832 and met the people living there, he was shocked by what he found.

"The climate is certainly wretched," he wrote. "Even in summer every day snow fell on the hills, and in the valleys there was rain with sleet. The thermometer generally stood about 45°F." Darwin described the skin of the Fuegians as "a dirty coppery red colour." Later, he was to meet and describe some of the tribes: "Among these central tribes the men generally have an otter skin, or some small scrap about as large as a pocket handkerchief, which is barely enough to cover their backs as low down as their loins. It is laced across the breast by strings and is shifted from side to side, depending on how the wind blows."

One group of Fuegians, who later approached Darwin's ship in a canoe, "were quite naked, and one full-grown woman was absolutely so. It was raining heavily and the sea spray trickled down her body. In another harbour not far distant, a woman who was suckling a recently born child came one day alongside the vessel and remained there out of curiosity while the sleet fell and thawed on her naked bosom and on the skin of her naked baby!"

Were these wretched people descendants of the Paleo-Indians of some 430 generations ago? It is hard to imagine people choosing such a harsh environment as a home. Some anthropologists have suggested that the southward movements of some Paleo-Indian groups may not have been voluntary, but forced. Settled groups may have been forced to move on southward by stronger and aggressive groups who displaced them. This has happened countless times in history. In this way the strong take and keep the good land and hunting grounds for themselves, forcing those who had settled it earlier to move on. We know this was the case after the Europeans arrived in America in the 1500s and 1600s and over the next two centuries forced the Indians off the choice regions of land.

Were there Paleo-Indians who had established settlements in America even earlier than the Clovis people? Trying to answer that question puts us in the middle of a lively argument among archaeologists. Some think that the Clovis people were the first arrivals. Others say no, there were pre-Clovis groups who came here at least 40,000 years ago. If so, who were they and how do we know about them?

# 6

## *The Argument Over Age*

In July 1966, C. R. Harington, a scientist with the National Museums of Canada, was searching for fossils along the banks of the Old Crow River in the Yukon. Each spring that gentle river goes on a spring-melt rampage, gouging out of its banks fossils by the thousands. While some are washed downstream, others are left exposed along its banks as the river lowers again. Recall from an earlier chapter that during the last glacial period Beringia and the Yukon were ice-free and served as an ideal route for hunter-gatherer groups from Asia to enter North America. The 3,000-square-mile (7,770-sq-km) Old Crow Basin supported dozens of different kinds of Ice Age game animals and must have been a hunter's paradise.

### Artifacts and Geofacts

Harington was delighted when his field assistant Peter Lord excitedly brought him part of a caribou leg bone. It was stained in such a way that made Harington think that the bone was very old indeed. But the interesting thing about the bone was that one end had a row of toothlike notches. This was no accident of nature or the work of an animal gnawing on the bone. The teeth were too even. Harington had seen carefully notched bones like this before. They are called fleshers and have long been used to scrape away the flesh clinging to the inside of the hide of a freshly killed animal. The bone flesher must have been fashioned by an early craftsman, but how early?

Imagine Harington's, and the rest of the Paleo-Indian scientific community's, surprise when radiocarbon dating of the caribou bone revealed an age of 27,000 years. Those archaeologists called the "early arrivalists," because they think that

Among the tools of bone used by the Paleo-Indians entering the New World were scrapers used to scrape away and clean the flesh of a skinned animal. The notched end of this ancient caribou bone was worked to provide teeth to serve as a scraper.

the Paleo-Indians came much earlier than 12,000 years ago, cheered the dating. They feel that evidence one day will show that Paleo-Indian groups were in America at least 30,000 years ago and possibly much earlier than 100,000 years ago. The "middle arrivalists" also welcomed the dating because it supports their view that the first Americans settled on our shores sometime between 12,000 and 30,000 years ago. A third group, called the "late arrivalists," were highly skeptical of the 27,000-year-old date. One reason is the tendency of archaeologists to accept radiocarbon dates with caution. Another, the find could have been an old bone picked up and notched by people living only a few thousand years ago, they argued. But why use an old brittle bone, the early arrivalists asked, when there were plenty of fresh caribou bones around? And so the argument continued until a second radiocarbon test was done, this time using a newer and somewhat more reliable technique. The revised age? A mere 1,350 years old!

Despite the young age for the scraper, archaeologists of the early arrivalist group think that many human-worked bones at Old Crow may indeed be at least 27,000 years old. (See Bonnichsen's statement in the Preface on page 9.) But all the while they are cautious, realizing the possibility of a bone appearing to be a tool could have been "fashioned" by an animal gnawing on it or by erosion, crushing, or other earth forces altering it. Such objects have come to be called geofacts.

### Sites Up to 21,000 Years Old
In North America archaeologists can point to more than thirty sites from Alaska to Texas and across to Georgia and eastern Canada where Clovis and similar fluted points have been found. There is general agreement that these sites are about 11,000 years old. There are about fifteen sites where carbon-14 dating has suggested ages from 11,000 to 18,000 years,

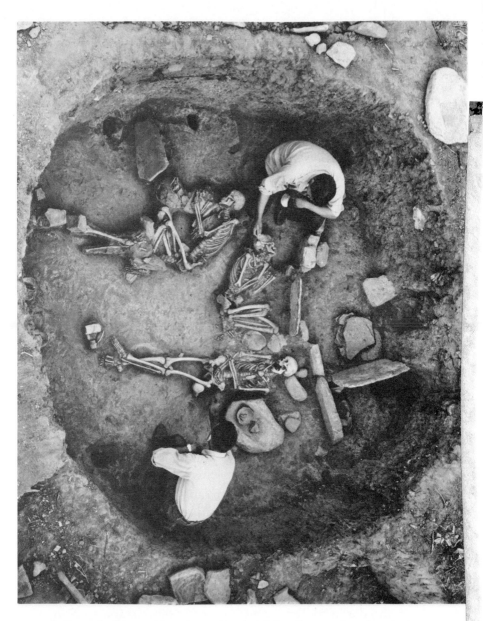

Anthropologists working at any site containing the remains of ancient man dig with great care in order to reveal the human remains or artifacts as nearly exactly as they were when buried. Shown here are four human burials and various artifacts uncovered at Mesa Verde, Colorado.

and there is general agreement about the accuracy of these ages. Seven more sites of that age have been found in South America, spread from the northern to the southern tip, and two others in Central America.

Working our way from younger to older sites, we will look into a few to find out what archaeologists have discovered.

In Virginia's Shenandoah Valley at the Thunderbird site archaeologists have found evidence that some Clovis culture groups may not have spent all their time as hunter-gatherers but had semipermanent camps where they settled for part of the year. The evidence for one such 11,000-year-old house, or houses, was a pattern of stains in the ground, called postmolds, left by posts that long ago rotted and chemically discolored the soil. Working with only bone and stone tools that would have been used 11,000 years ago, archaeologist Errett Callahan reconstructed what he thinks the original house might have been like. It was large enough to serve as an efficient, heated structure for about thirty people. Northward are a half dozen more Clovis-culture settlements, one in Nova Scotia where archaeologists have found 3,200 stone tools and charcoal hearth remains dated from 10,600 years ago.

Near the tip of South America, in Chile, at the site called Fell's Cave there are convincing signs that the cave was used as a shelter 11,000 years ago. Distinctive fluted points with bases shaped like a fish tail have been found. There also is evidence that these people had tamed wild dogs. Similar evidence of domesticated dogs has been found at Old Crow sites. About 250 miles (400 km) north in Argentina another cave, at Los Toldos, served as a shelter for other groups of Paleo-Indians who hunted wild llama some 12,600 years ago.

Near present-day Sarasota, Florida, at a site known as Little Salt Spring, a scuba-diving archaeologist revealed a

12,000-year-old drama. An Indian slipped into a large, deep hole and fell 90 feet (27 m) into the water of an enormous spring, and survived. He managed to swim to the edge and onto a shelf of rock at about water level. From time to time debris and other animals apparently had been claimed by the large sinkhole, from which there was no escape. Judging from evidence found at the site, the Indian discovered that he had company—a giant land tortoise that had tumbled into the spring earlier. The unlucky Indian speared the tortoise with a stick and cooked the animal, probably the Indian's last meal. The remains of the tortoise were found resting on fire-baked clay along with the stick, which was radiocarbon dated at 12,000 years old. The bones of other animals also were found, including those of an extinct sloth. In time, Little Salt Spring certainly will give up many more secrets.

Moving southward across the Caribbean Sea to the northern tip of South America we find a site called Taima-Taima on the coast of Venezuela. Here by a water hole archaeologist José Cruxent dug up the skeletons of four mastodons. Among the bones of one was an El Jobo bifacial projectile point. He found it amid the bones in the position of the animal's bladder. This suggested to him that the mastodon was killed by spear poisoning, a method used to this day by African elephant poachers. Radiocarbon dating of the site showed an age of 13,000 years. Later, Canadian archaeologists examined the site and found another El Jobo point lodged in the bladder region of another animal. Further radiocarbon dating confirmed an age of 13,000 years.

An interesting sidelight of the Taima-Taima find is the El Jobo point, which is leaf-shaped and not fluted. It seems to have been designed as a spear tip and shows evidence of pressure flaking as well as striking. Is it possible that these hunters in South America had learned to craft their points from people of the Clovis culture? Or did the two cultures develop their stone points independently over a distance of several thousands of miles? The Canadian researchers favor independent development.

Almost halfway down South America in the mountain region of Peru near the coast is the site of Pikimachay—Flea Cave. The cave is six stories high and covers half a city block. Archaeologists studying the cave have found the bones of giant ground sloths, giant cats, horses, camels, and deer. They also found special areas that had been used for butchering and working bone and flint tools. Radiocarbon dating shows that Paleo-Indians occupied the cave at least 14,000 years ago, and possibly as long ago as 25,000 years, according to archaeologist Richard MacNeish.

In south central Chile is another site of similar age known as Monte Verde. Of special interest are wooden house structures well preserved by a bog. Mastodon bones and stone artifacts along with seeds and stocks of certain edible plants also were found. Thomas Dillehay of the University of Kentucky says that Monte Verde is the most complete and best preserved wooden house site yet discovered. These people may well have led settled lives in permanent dwellings and practiced limited farming from 12,000 to 14,000 years ago.

Dennis Stanford has uncovered a wealth of Paleo-Indian materials at the Dutton site on the Colorado plains, once an Ice Age water hole. At the upper layer of the dig was unmistakable evidence of people of the Clovis culture, including Clovis points. Deeper down were the remains of earlier people who seem to have used only tools of bone, similar to bone tools found at Old Crow. Stanford feels that the Dutton site may prove to be as old as 20,000 years.

About 40 miles (64 km) southwest of Pittsburgh is an especially rich site known as the Meadowcroft Rockshelter, an area used for shelter from prehistoric times until the 1700s. So far 3.5 million artifacts have been found. The remains of what looked like a basket made of tree bark was radiocarbon-dated to an age of about 21,000 years. The remains have been recovered from eleven different levels and include human bones. One of the more interesting finds was a Clovislike point but without the flute. Archaeologist James M. Adovasio of the University of Pittsburgh thinks that the bifacial point "may be ancestral to the Clovis point." Another like it that may be 14,500 years old was found in the Wilson Butte Cave in Idaho.

### Sites About 30,000 Years Old

Farther south, in Mexico, Juan Armenta Camacho has worked a site called Valsequillo where he uncovered many artifacts. Among them were mastodon bones that bear sketches of Ice Age animals scratched into the bone with a sharp point. Over the years, digging a 100-foot (30-m)-deep trench has produced the remains of Ice Age bison, camels, mastodons, horses, and mammoths. Of special interest was evidence of ancient butchers cutting up a mastodon. The level at which the butchered mastodon was found points to an age of about 22,000 years.

Another archaeological team led by José Luis Lorenzo and digging at the nearby site of Tlapacoya found the bones of deer and black bear associated with the charred remains of hearths also dated at 22,000 years old. Radiocarbon dating of a buried tree trunk on top of a cutting blade of obsidian gave a similar age.

The last middle arrivalist site we will examine before moving on to early arrivalist sites is an interesting one in Brazil's state of Piauí. There are nearly 200 limestone rock shelters and caves where people have sheltered and lived for many thousands of years. The Brazilian archaeologist Niède Guidon was especially interested in the cave named Toca do Boqueirão da Pedra Furada. The walls bear paintings of Ice Age hunters in action. From time to time over the centuries pieces of rock bearing part of a painting have chipped off. The oldest layers of soil in which some of the chips have been found have been radiocarbon dated from 17,000 to more than 30,000 years. These dates are evidence of Paleo-Indian occupation of the cave at the upper limit of the middle arrivalists age bracket of between about 12,000 and 30,000 years.

In the next chapter we will push the history of Paleo-Indians still further back in time by sampling some of the evidence offered by early arrivalist archaeologists.

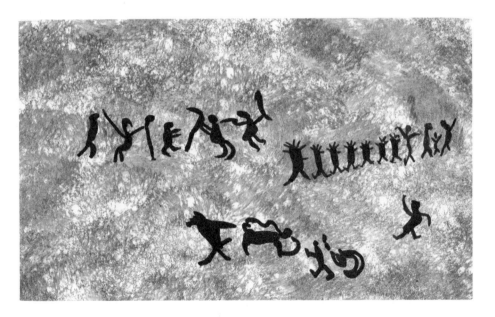

Paleo-Indian artists in Brazil made cave paintings, paint chips of which have been dated between 17,000 and 30,000 years old. The sketch here, a copy of the original art, is said to show hunting activity.

# 7
# *What the Early Arrivalists Claim*

Before we explore some of the sites uncovered by the early arrivalists we should take a brief look at part of the story anthropologists in many parts of the world are piecing together about our human ancestory. This will be helpful since the dates some of the early arrivalists are coming up with take us back more than 100,000 years. What were "people" like then?

## Who Were The First Human Beings?

About 700,000 years ago there were scattered populations so much like modern people that anthropologists include them in the scientific class—called a genus—*Homo* (which means "man"). But because there are important differences between us and them, they are given the second name—called a species—*erectus* (which means "upright"). Present-day humans are classed as *Homo sapiens* (which means "wise man"). All of the Paleo-Indian remains discovered so far show that these early Americans were fully modern members of *Homo sapiens*.

Although *Homo erectus* was well on the way to evolving into the species *sapiens,* these people had skulls with powerful jaws and large faces with a low brow bone. *Homo erectus* was muscular and powerful. With their large brains they may have developed speech. These people survived for some 400,000 years before they were replaced by other human beings. Their remains have been found in North Africa, Germany, Hungary, and China.

About 300,000 years ago Africa and parts of Eurasia had human populations closely resembling people living in those regions today. However, the head shape of those earlier people sets them apart from modern people. Their skulls were a bit longer than ours, they had large faces, a bony ridge over their brow, slight chins, and powerful jaws. Over those 300,000 years to the present, evolution changed the head shape of these people by making the large brow ridge smaller and enlarging the chin, for example.

We know of a few *Homo sapiens* fossils older than 200,000 years—two from France, one from England, and one from Germany.

Fossil evidence shows that around 100,000 years ago there were populations of large-jawed people known as Neanderthals in many places—from Gibraltar across Europe into the Near East and into central Asia. They lived in caves or in the open in tents made of animal skins. About five feet tall, they were strong and had large bones. About 35,000 years ago Neanderthals mysteriously died out and were replaced by Cro-Magnon, or modern man. This happened in South Africa about 60,000 years ago. Cro-Magnon types were living in southeast Asia about 40,000 years ago, and in Europe about 30,000 years ago. The changeover from Neanderthal to Cro-Magnon took place over a period of about 5,000 years.

The point of mentioning the age of modern man and his ancestors is that some researchers push the date of arrival of the Paleo-Indians back to a time earlier than the appearance of Cro-Magnon (about 60,000 years ago). Since the Paleo-Indians were modern human types, they could not have been in America earlier than 60,000 years ago. Simply because modern human types did not exist earlier than that.

*Homo sapiens* is the sole remaining human species today. Although we all belong to one species, there are different races of us. Most biologists recognize three races—Caucasoid (light-skinned), Negroid (dark-skinned), and Mongoloid (intermediate with high cheekbones). There are five races if the Australian aborigines and American Indians are counted as separate races. Around the end of the last Ice Age some 11,000 years ago the total world population was about five million people, five times the present population of the state of Maine. Today's total world population is about five billion. That is a thousand times more people than there were when Beringia was last exposed.

## Early Arrivalist Sites

Among the more recent of the early arrivalist sites is one on California's Santa Rosa Island off the coast of Los Angeles. The island is well known among paleontologists for the remains of extinct dwarf mammoths. These small elephants stood only about six feet high at the shoulders. Geologist John Woolley discovered the site and uncovered many ancient bones and primitive stone tools. Unfortunately, none of the tools was clearly found in unquestionable association with any of the bones. If one of the stone points had been embedded in a rib bone, for instance, then radiocarbon dating of the rib would show not only the mammoth's age but the age of the stone point as well. No such luck.

Then in 1976 Woolley discovered what he concluded was an ancient fireplace. It was an area about 10 feet (3 m) across and contained bones, tools, and charcoal from ancient cooking fires. Charcoal samples taken from the hearth and radiocarbon dated showed an age of about 40,000 years.

Another find along the California coast, this one by Jeffrey Bada of the University of California at San Diego, revealed human bones thought by some to be about 48,000 years old. Human remains thought to be about 50,000 years old were discovered by geologist Archie MacS. Stalker along the ice-free corridor near Taber, Alberta, Canada. The bones were those of a Paleo-Indian infant known by archaeologists as the Taber child. Neither the 48,000- nor 50,000-year-old date has been accepted by archaeologists. The problem is not a lack of Paleo-Indian bones but a reliable way of dating them, one that everyone agrees on. There is the Laguna Girl, the L.A. Man, the Del Mar Man, and other Paleo-Indian remains. In one case four different dating methods produced four different ages for a single find. The dates ranged from 10,000 to 23,600 years.

Geologists studying the rock layers in the Old Crow region of the Yukon think that some artifacts come from layers that point to an age of at least 60,000 years. But again, there are too many ifs to make such a claim with certainty.

The further that dates indicating the presence of Paleo-Indians in the Americas are pushed back, the less certain they seem to be. California's Calico Hills site in the Mojave Desert is an example. In 1963 Ruth Simpson, an archaeologist with the San Bernardino County Museum in Redlands, California, found what she thought might be crude stone tools near Calico. At the time, the late British archaeologist Louis Leakey was a visiting professor at the University of California at Riverside. She invited Leakey to visit the site with her and

58

examine the "tools." Leakey studied them carefully and said that they seemed to be very much like the many primitive stone tools he had dug up in East Africa. In 1964 the National Geographic Society provided money to start a dig at the Calico Hills site.

The site has been an active one since the dig began. So far, more than 10,000 artifacts have been found, many of which Leakey felt, and Simpson continues to feel, are tools unmistakably worked by ancient craftsmen. While some archaeologists agree, others say that the tools are nothing more than geofacts. All agree that the site is, indeed, very old. Radiocarbon dating of a mammoth tusk indicated an age older than 40,000 years. The site is a huge gravel deposit which geologists call an alluvial fan. These fans are caused by streams or rivers depositing sediments in heaps when the stream or river suddenly is slowed down by a ravine or mountain, for example. The layered deposits in an alluvial fan often become mixed so that remains of different age are sometimes found at the same level of a dig. The crushing action of the rocks in an alluvial fan also can cause pressure flaking and so produce a geofact that might be mistaken for an artifact. Simpson, however, claims that she can distinguish between the two in most cases.

When the dig had reached a depth of about 23 feet (7 m) in 1968, a semicircle of stones was found. Leakey was not surprised by this find and suspected that it might be the remains of a hearth. Tests made sometime later cast serious doubt that the arrangement of stones was a hearth. Possibly the deliberate work of ancient man, the semicircle has yet to be explained.

In 1970 the San Bernardino County Museum invited scholars from all over the world to attend a conference and examine the site and its artifacts (or geofacts). Some agreed with Leakey and Simpson that the site probably had been occupied by toolmaking people some 200,000 years ago. Others did not. If it had been, then the craftsmen who worked those tools most likely were *Homo sapiens* who crossed over from northern Asia during a glacial period much earlier than the most recent one. If so, then where are the human remains?

Among the doubters of the Calico Hills site is Stanford, one of the world's most respected field archaeologists. "I just don't see a whole lot of good evidence," he says. "And if in the end [those archaeologists favoring an early arrival] are wrong about their theories of an early occupation, then they may have done a lot of damage to the reputation of archaeology. You have got to be careful." Today the Calico site is an outdoor archaeological museum open to the public. If you visit it you will see the meticulous way archaeologists work a site. You will also see the semicircle of stones and artifacts, or geofacts, left exactly where the diggers uncovered them.

That Paleo-Indian cultures were well settled in both North and South America at least 11,000 years ago is beyond doubt. But how much earlier they may have made the New World their home is a puzzle that dozens of archaeologists are trying to solve. All are waiting for that one find that every one can agree to and that will clearly establish early man in the New World 50,000 or more years ago. One writer has described the search for early man in the New World as "the most sweeping manhunt ever staged."

If we are not able to pin down the arrival times of the first Paleo-Indians, we are on much firmer ground when we trace their later movements across North America and down South America's west coast. The clues are fresher and much more reliable.

# 8

# The Spread of Paleo-Indian Cultures

They came in waves century after century following the last glacial period, crossing over from Beringia and pressing ever farther southward and eastward until they had populated the Arctic and North and South America. They were the Paleo-Indians and by the year 1500 their descendants had developed hundreds of cultures and their total population had grown to some forty million. These descendants of the Paleo-Indians include the Mayas, Aztecs, Eskimos, Mohawks, Navajos, Zunis, Senecas, and dozens of other North American Indian groups.

The early American descendants of the Paleo-Indians lived in bands numbering anywhere from a few dozen to a few hundred or more. In North America alone there were enough such groups to have spoken at least 200 languages at the time the Spanish and English arrived. Although each language was distinct, some were similar enough to be grouped into language families. For example, the Iroquoian language family included the Seneca, Mohawk, and Cherokee languages. While several present-day Southwest Indian groups have al-

61

most identical cultures, they speak languages that belong to four different families. All of the languages spoken by Native Americans at the time of Columbus's voyage to America evolved here in the New World, arising from very old and unknown language bases. The Eskimo-Aleut language family seems to be the most recent arrival in the New World and may have evolved from a much older Asian tongue. Of the several hundred languages spoken by those early Americans, all were unwritten except for one—the Mayan language.

### From Hunting to Farming

The ways of life of the early Americans differed nearly as much as their languages. Some continued an existence as hunter-gatherers, wandering about killing what game they could find and eating seasonal berries, wild fruit, and nuts. Others lived a more settled life in semipermanent shelters of wood or animal skins. When certain groups began to grow useful food plants from seed, their lives changed dramatically. The first to do so in the Americas probably lived in the highlands of Mexico about 8,000 or more years ago. They learned to cultivate maize (corn), which soon became the single most important food plant in the New World. By 5,000 years ago Indian farmers in central Mexico also were growing beans, squash, and other plants. Halfway around the world in Iraq, groups were growing wheat and barley about this time. About 4,000 years later the Chinese along the Yellow River learned to grow millet, and later rice. So agriculture was discovered independently and at different times in many parts of the world. Those groups that remained hunter-gatherers most likely did so because agriculture requires more labor than hunting and gathering food.

The practice of growing food plants instead of simply gathering them spread rapidly among neighboring populations and was a cultural revolution for those who practiced the art. Life was no longer only a matter of survival. Thought could be given to other matters—the development of different kinds of weapons and tools, more elaborate basketry, clothing, and ornaments, better houses, and more elaborate ceremonies, and time to develop intellectual skills such as astronomy and mathematics.

Agriculture most likely arose out of a need. Dwindling supplies of game as a result of increased hunting by an ever-growing population must have made people more and more dependent on food plants as a source of nutrition. Also, climate change in temperature and rainfall some 12,000 years ago had started the extinction of the mammoths, mastodons, giant sloths, horses, and camels, for example. At first, farming groups probably had several seasonal "farms" which they visited in turn as various food plants ripened throughout the year. Mexico's Tehuacán Valley and Peru's Ayacucho Valley are two such regions that must have made ideal seasonal farmlands. Only later did these early farming groups settle down in one place, claiming certain areas as their own and defending them against intruders.

## Social Change Brought By Farming

Settlement meant new kinds of social organization and larger local populations to share in the large amount of labor needed in agriculture compared with that needed by those following a nomadic hunter-gatherer existence. It also meant the need of a reliable water supply for crops, drinking, and sanitation, hence elaborate irrigation systems such as those great ditches built by people of the Hohokam culture in central Arizona, the canal system of people living along the Peruvian coast, and aqueducts made by the Incas of Cuzco, which still stand. Such massive engineering efforts required much labor.

A group's control over its own cared-for food plants meant that a surplus of food could be stored for use during times of need, during periods of drought, for instance. Drought was common in the southwestern United States and in Mesoamerica and probably was partly the cause of some cultural centers being suddenly and mysteriously abandoned. An ample and predictable supply of food also freed certain individuals from the need to gather food. They could then become specialists and develop skills in arts and crafts, which further enriched their culture.

But surplus food had to be protected from dampness, insects, and rodents. Pottery storage jars were the answer. Need stimulates invention. As the practice of agriculture spread northward and eastward from central Mexico, so did pottery making. But the spread of agriculture, like the process of its development, did not take place overnight. It took many generations of accidental discoveries, learning methods of plant and seed selection by trial and error, and for the selected food plants to improve genetically so that they developed tastier and larger fruits than earlier varieties.

By about 4,000 years ago in central Mexico small villages of about a dozen houses built on 5 or so acres (2 ha) were common. Each house was about 10 by 18 feet (3 by 6 m), and was made of woven branches supported by a wood frame and covered by sunbaked mud. And each had its own grave plot and a pit for food storage. During this Pre-Classic Period trade was common along well-traveled routes crossing hundreds of miles. Tooled leather and cutting blades made of obsidian were among commonly traded items.

## Pre-Classic Mesoamerica

The first major civilization in the New World was one called the Olmec. Four Olmec sites have been uncovered. Three are near the gulf coast of southern Mexico: San Lorenzo, dated at 1250 B.C. to 900 B.C.; La Venta, the largest site, 1100 B.C. to 400 B.C.; and Tres Zapotes, another large center, 500 B.C. to 100 B.C. The fourth, Copalillo, is a recently discovered site along the Pacific coast that had stone architecture as early as 1200 B.C.

Olmec astronomers seem to have developed the first New World calendar. The Olmecs are known for the huge 20-ton stone heads carved out of basalt quarried from more than 25 miles (40 km) away. To date, thirteen of the heads, thought to be sculptures of Olmec rulers, have been found. They also built large mounds of earth, such as that at La Venta, and dug

Matthew Stirling, of the Smithsonian Institution, was a major scholar of the Olmec culture. Here, at Tres Zapotes, he measures one of the colossal stone helmeted heads carved out of basalt by the Olmec. This head is 6 feet (1.8 meters) high, 18 feet (5.5 meters) around, and weighs 10 tons. Some of the heads weighed up to 20 tons.

extensive drainage systems. Some anthropologists think that the Olmec culture was an interaction sphere, a blend or sharing of several similar cultures of small regional populations. The Olmec people ruled from El Salvador in the south northward into central Mexico. They carried on a lively trade in serpentine, obsidian, and jade and their influence was to be felt in later cultures. The great centers of San Lorenzo and La Venta met violent and destructive ends, their monuments and altars battered and broken. Archaeologist David C. Grove thinks that the destruction may have been done by the Olmecs themselves at the death of one of their rulers. This Pre-Classic Period of Mesoamerica ended around A.D. 300 and gave way to what is called the Classic Period that was to span some 600 years.

## The Classic Period

By the beginning of the Classic Period the proud city of Teotihuacán in central Mexico could boast of a population of about 200,000. This made it the largest cultural center in the New World. The enormous Pyramid of the Sun, measuring 700 feet (213 m) on each side and standing 243 feet (74 m) high, was the city's overpowering central feature. Requiring nearly a million tons of earth, it was larger than the great Egyptian pyramid at Giza. Pyramids by the thousands were to dot the Mexican landscape over the centuries. They were used for both religious and political purposes. Two things made Teotihuacán a thriving center—an extensive irrigation system and control of the major source of volcanic glass called obsidian and used to make elaborate cutting blades. After about 350 years of splendor, Teotihuacán for some unknown reason was deserted by its people and by the year 750 the once-proud city was all but abandoned.

As Teotihuacán slipped into decline, to the south the

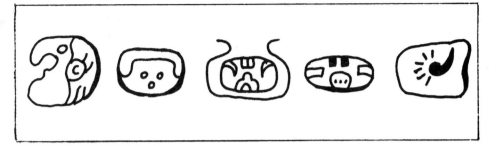

When Spanish Catholic missionary Bishop Diego de Landa asked the Maya to draw their alphabet for him, they included these pictographs of their writing. Left to right A (AAC); E; C(KE); T; and B(BE).

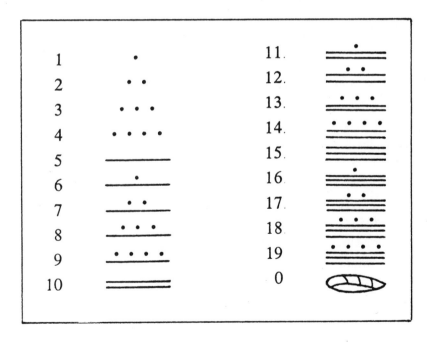

How to count in Maya

Maya culture, which had begun around 500 B.C., flowered and came to dominate the land for a thousand years. Cities such as Uxmal, Chichén Itzá, Tikal, and Copán became important centers bustling with trade and producing splendid works of art. Tikal's population probably was about 40,000. In all there were about sixty Maya cities and a population probably around three million. The Maya occupied the Mesoamerican regions now called the Yucatán Peninsula, Guatemala, Belize, and southernmost Mexico, in all a bit larger than New England today. There were several local populations organized into city-states that often were at war with each other.

The Maya were excellent architects, mathematicians, and astronomers. Their mathematics surpassed that of the Greeks and Romans. Knowing when certain stars appeared at certain times of the year was important in order to keep track of the seasons and to know just when to begin the spring planting and fall harvest. Such knowledge of the heavens, associated with the gods, usually was kept secret by the politically powerful astronomer-priests. This was true also in ancient Egypt and Mesopotamia. The Maya also were able to predict eclipses and developed a remarkably accurate solar calendar that gave the length of the year as 365.2420 days compared with today's 365.2422 days. They had a special calendar to keep track of religious events. And, as mentioned earlier, the Maya were the only New World culture to develop a system of writing.

Like their ancestors before them, the Maya mysteriously abandoned their cities from about the year A.D. 800 to A.D. 900. Some scholars suspect that the populations of these cities had become too large to be fed by the limited farmland crops. So gradually people began leaving the cities to take up life in smaller groups more manageable nutritionally. Other scholars have suggested revolution as the cause. According to one, "In city after city the ruling group was driven out or, more probably, massacred by the dependent peasants, and power then passed to peasant leaders and small-town witch doctors." The magnificent Maya culture lasted about 1,000 years and rivaled that of ancient Egypt. Today there are about two million Maya still working the land of their ancestors and speaking their language. There were other Mesoamerican cultures at the time of the Maya, but none as great. Among them were the Zapotecs who lived in southwestern Mexico and built fortresses on hilltops and constructed a sacred temple at Monte Albán. Monte Albán probably ranked as a major city with its

The Maya did not construct an arch with a keystone. Instead they built corbeled arches, closing the gap at the top of the arch with a long flat stone rather than making the gap narrow still more until it could be filled in by dropping a keystone into the final slot. The corbeled archway here is part of a wall at Tulum, Yucatan.

astronomical observatory, monumental buildings, ball courts, and agricultural terraces.

## The Post-Classic Period

The weakening and failure of the Maya centers marked the end of the Classic Period of Mesoamerica in the year 900. The Maya were replaced by another culture known as the Toltecs from Tula, a city north of Teotihuacán. They were a warlike people and among their conquests was their occupation of the elegant Maya city of Chichén Itzá.

The Aztecs were the next, and last, great builders before the arrival of the Spanish conquerors in the 1500s. Warlike nomad hunters, the Aztecs came southward from northern Mexico and established themselves in the Valley of Mexico in the 1200s. They were quick to learn the ways of agriculture from their neighbors and by a century and a half later had built the amazing city of Tenochtitlán by Lake Texcoco, just east of present-day Mexico City. It was among the world's largest cities with a population of some 200,000 and consisted of palaces, temples, and lesser dwellings. Instead of having streets, a network of canals was ever busy with canoe traffic. When the Spanish invaders first gazed on it in 1519 they did so with unbelieving eyes.

The Aztecs' lives were dominated by religious beliefs based on numerous bloodthirsty and demanding gods. According to their religion, an agreement long ago had been made between the Aztecs and their chief gods. The gods would provide a rich supply of food and maintain order in nature for as long as the Aztecs performed human sacrifices. At special times they cut out the hearts of living victims— sometimes their own people, other times slaves and warriors taken in battle. Parts of the sacrificed victims were then eaten in a stew containing corn.

The Aztecs were easily defeated by Hernán Cortés and his small band of conquerors who arrived on Mexico's gulf coast in 1519. They persuaded allies of the Aztecs to join forces with them. So strengthened, the Spanish easily overthrew the Aztec rulers. The rest of the story was one of destruction of what the Spanish disliked about the Aztec culture and the looting of what they did like. Part of Cortés's systematic destruction was the draining of the irrigated farmlands in the Valley of Mexico. Several years later, in 1562, the Spanish Catholic missionary Diego de Landa was appalled by the idea of the Indians worshiping many gods. At the time there were

The Aztecs recorded their ideas of time and the universe in this 12-foot (3.7-meter) stone "calendar." At center is the sun surrounded by fire serpents that carry it across the sky daily. The eighteen-month Aztec year is represented by the twenty symbols forming a circle around the fire serpents.

71

many Maya manuscripts describing the history of the Maya people and their religion and language. In the name of Christianity, de Landa ordered the manuscripts and books burned, the destruction of temples, and the slaughter of thousands of pagan believers. The devastation of Aztec culture marked the end of the Post-Classic Period of the Mesoamerican people.

## The Mysterious Chavín de Huántar

The next dig takes us southward to South America's coastal country of Peru which borders the Pacific coast. Nearly 3,000 years ago, around 850 B.C., the first major Andean culture flowered, remained for some 600 years, and then mysteriously disappeared. It was located inland from the sea 10,000 feet (3,100 m) up in the north-central highlands of Peru and is known as Chavín de Huántar. These people did not have a written language and so could not keep records. Although they never invented the wheel—no Indian group in the Americas ever did—they excelled in engineering and architecture. They also carried religion and art to impressive heights.

Chavín was a religious center, possibly a holy city, that attracted villagers from several days' journey to attend rituals and make offerings of food, pottery, and other items to the gods. Terraced farmland and an elaborate stone temple where animal, and probably human, sacrifices were made marked the center of this strange religious cult of the supernatural. Their nightmarish gods were half-animal and half-human, including jaguars, alligators, and snakes blended with part-human forms. Some scholars think that such blending of animal features represented a blending of characters such as courage, strength, and skill. These fanciful figures may have been called up and worshiped at ceremonies during which members of the cult chewed coca leaves and may have taken drugs that open the mind to strange sensations. To this day Peruvian Indians living in the region of Chavín claim that animallike gods live among the peaks of the Andes. Chavín priests traveled far and wide to win new worshipers, until eventually all of Peru came under their domain. Then around 200 B.C. the culture of Chavín disappeared, mysteriously and without signs of violence. Never again was that fertile valley nestled among the peaks of the Andes to become a major cultural center.

## The Chimu of Chan Chan and the Incas

Some 1,500 years before the Aztecs built Tenochtitlán, a strange cultural group known as the Chimu was thriving in the city of Chan Chan along the northern coast of Peru. Their empire stretched for more than 600 miles (960 km) along the coast. They lived within a walled city, had irrigation canals and a social system that included taxation and social classes of ruling nobility, expert craftsmen, and peasant farmers and fishermen. Their ceramic sculpture and vividly painted pottery record scenes from war and hunting.

Among Chimu gods was the powerful Si, goddess of the Moon, who controlled the weather, agriculture, and who punished thieves. Superstition, religion, and politics for the Chimu were mixed as a single belief system. If the patient of a medicine man died because of what today is called "malpractice," the medicine man was killed. A person guilty of civil disobedience was buried alive with the bones of traitors. Unmarried people caught having sex were thrown off a cliff to their death. A person caught stealing, along with his father and brothers, could be executed by the person he stole from. The Chimu did not have a written language and their spoken language has been lost. As a society, they were highly organized, powerful, and efficient, yet around 1460 they were conquered in battle by South America's other major culture, the Incas to the south.

73

## The Incas

The Chimu ruler, Minchancaman, was taken captive and moved to the Inca capital of Cuzco. The Incas looted Chan Chan, carrying off anything of value to them. The marauding Spaniards later finished off the city. They even changed the course of the Moche River to destroy the nearby pyramids of the sun and moon. The Incas took over many of the ways of the Chimu social system, including their high respect for law, and punishment. Although the Incas learned from the Chimu culture and adopted much of it, they failed to improve on it. Much the same thing happened when the Romans conquered the superior culture of ancient Greece.

It would be a mistake to think that all of the Mesoamerican and South American ancient cultures were concentrated in the city-states described. There were countless smaller, village populations that dotted the countryside. Most of these, however, fell under control of whatever nearby city-state happened to be in power at the time. The people making up these small outlying groups were forced to pay taxes in the form of crops, pottery, or whatever materials or skills they were able to contribute.

The various cultures of Mesoamerica and South America reached social, religious, technological, and political heights realized by few of the many cultures that evolved in North America. It is because of the splendid achievements of the Central and South American descendants of the Paleo-Indians that we have spent so much time with them in this chapter. While they were building their massive pyramids, fine temples, and evolving complex political and social systems, what was happening in the north in what was to become Canada and the United States?

People of the Nazca culture along the coast of Peru were weaving cloth of wool into intricate designs as early as the second century A.D. The fragment of a border done in regularly repeated stem stitch is shown here.

# 9

# *The Eskimos and Indians of the Southwest*

By the year 1492 the descendants of the Paleo-Indians had fashioned hundreds of cultures and their populations had adapted to many environmental nooks and crannies—the Arctic, the seacoast, the tropics, humid or arid zones, and the lowlands to mountain settlements at 15,000-foot (4,570-m) heights in South America. Their intelligence and invention propelled them into agriculture, city planning, architecture, civil engineering, and made them potters, painters, metallurgists, weavers, dyers, and poets. In the previous chapter we saw many of their attainments in Mesoamerica and Peru. In this and the following chapters we will find out about their accomplishments to the north, in what is today the United States and Canada.

## The Eskimos: Inuits and Aleuts

The Eskimos—known by their native name Inuits—and the closely related Aleuts were recent arrivals from Asia to the New World. They settled in the region of Alaska only some 6,000 or so years ago. The Aleuts are offshoots of the Inuit.

They settled in the Aleutian Islands about 3,000 years ago. These islands number about seventy and are the flattened peaks of undersea volcanoes that form a thousand-mile-long arc southwest of the peninsula of Alaska.

Physically these two groups differ from the Indians of both North and South America. They closely resemble modern Asian populations, which is not true of any Indian groups. Eskimo cultures also are different from those of Indian groups and reflect their dependency for food, clothing, and tools not on the land but from the sea. According to T. D. Stewart, an anthropologist formerly with Washington's National Museum of Natural History, "By catching sea birds, fish, seals, walruses, and whales, they obtain meat for food, oil for light and heat, skin (including fur and feathers) for clothing, boat coverings, bags, thongs, sinews, and bones and ivory for [tools and artistic carvings]."

The spread of the Eskimos was rapid and broad, ranging from Siberia eastward across the Arctic to Greenland, a distance well over 6,000 miles (9,600 km). Another reason for thinking that the Eskimos are recent arrivals is their language. As mentioned in an earlier chapter, the many thousands of years of cultural development of descendants of the Paleo-Indians were enough time for many very different language families and individual languages to develop. This has not been so with the Eskimos. The Danish explorer Knud Rasmussen, who spoke the Eskimoan language, once traveled from Greenland westward to Alaska without once having trouble talking with the many Eskimo groups he visited. The 1,000 years since the separation of Eskimo groups living in the east from groups living in the west had not been long enough for their stock language to splinter into separate languages. But when Rasmussen met the Aleuts, he was not able to understand them and they could not understand the Eskimoan he spoke. The Aleuts and Eskimos had parted ways some 3,000 or more years ago, a long enough time for the Aleuts' dialect of Eskimoan to have evolved into a language of their own.

The Eskimos' lack of a prominent nose and relatively short fingers are thought to be adaptations to a cold environment since such features reduce heat loss and so lessen the chance of frostbite. Their regulation of heat loss from the body in general is another adaptation to the cold. South American Indian populations living high in the mountains and at extreme southern latitudes also have this adaptation, although populations living in warmer climates do not. Because the Eskimos' have been influenced by European and American ways since the 1930s, they have become a less healthy people. According to Stewart, their resulting change in diet has been the main cause. In place of sea mammals and fish, rich in nutrients and requiring hard use of the teeth, they came to depend on soft, manufactured food. As a result, tooth decay, for instance, became common.

It wasn't until 1741, some 200 years after the Spaniards plundered their way through Mesoamerica, that a Russian expedition sailing from Asia stumbled onto the Aleutian Islands. The total Aleut population around 200 years ago probably reached about 20,000 but today they number fewer than 1,000. Continued contact with the Russians all but wiped them out. In the words of anthropologist T. P. Bank: "Adventurers, thieves, exiles, murderers and princes alike set out to plunder this remote region of its treasure. A tide of greed, cruelty and bloodshed swept over the Aleutian Islands. The Aleuts fought back, but they were overwhelmed by the superior weapons of the Russian hunters. Whole villages were wiped out; the population was decimated not only by guns but also by smallpox, measles, tuberculosis and pneumonia."

Skilled hunters of seals, whales, and sea lions, the Aleuts wasted nothing of a killed whale towed ashore. They ate its meat and burned its fat for heat and light. Its ribs and jawbones became building materials for their underground houses of sod. Its shoulder blades were made into tables while its small sections of backbone became chairs. Some bone ends were polished as plates, and other bones were fashioned into harpoon tips and daggers. The intestines were formed into rain parkas and light-admitting windows, its sinews became thread and cord, and its teeth were carved into ornaments, arrowheads, and needles.

In navigation and seamanship, the Aleuts surpassed all other Eskimo groups. The eastern Aleuts made mummies of their dead. They scooped out all the soft internal organs and stuffed the body cavity with moss. The body was then covered in bird skins or fur, tied and hidden in a cave, or propped up in a natural position among the coastal rocks as if looking out to sea.

What is left of the once-proud culture of the Aleuts today? According to Bank: "It is a picture all too familiar to anthropologists: a once-thriving, independent people, admirably disciplined for life in a rigorous environment, now impoverished, diseased and spiritually weakened, its ancient culture all but destroyed. The story might serve as a lesson to us. But it is probably too late to save the southernmost of our Eskimos."

### Indians of the Southwest

About 5,000 years ago, soon after the first Eskimo settlements, several southwestern Indian cultures existed and were in touch with each other and probably in touch with Mexican cultures to the south. The groups were hunter-gatherers and remained so until some 3,500 years ago when they seem to have learned agriculture and pottery making from their southern neighbors.

These many small cultures were to develop into three cultural provinces, or groups. The two major ones were the Anasazi (a Navajo word meaning "old people") and the Hohokam (a Pima word meaning "those who have gone"). The third is the Mogollon, named after the Mogollon Mountains. All three lie within the regions of Colorado, Utah, Nevada, Arizona, and New Mexico and were in communication with each other and with lesser groups through the trading of raw materials, finished products, and the exchange of ideas.

The Anasazi had their roots in Paleo-Indian stock some 9,000 years old. Seven thousand years ago they were hunter-gatherers, and by 3,000 years ago they had learned to grow maize from their southern neighbors. They reached their cultural peak between the years 900 and 1100. By this time they had carved their presence in New Mexico's 10-mile (16-km)-long Chaco Canyon by constructing eight major apartment-building complexes called pueblos, the first such buildings in the New World.

Some of the structures reached five stories high and housed hundreds of people. The most famous is one called Pueblo Bonito, which sprawled over 3 acres (1 ha) of land. Timbers for support beams had to be carried from forests 25 miles (40 km) away. Some 200,000 such beams were used in the construction. Hundreds of miles of roadways linked Chaco Canyon with smaller outlying villages. The Anasazi also built dams and canals to trap and channel rainwater to their gardens of maize, beans, and squash, food which they supplemented with game killed by spears and the bow and arrow. During the 1100s drought and poor hunting seem to have made the canyon uninhabitable and brought the flourishing Anasazi culture to an end. Modern-day descendants of the

The crumbled remains of Pueblo Bonito ("Beautiful Village") lie baking in New Mexico's Chaco Canyon. The canyon has 18 major ruins, of which Pueblo Bonito is the largest. All were built from about A.D. 919 to 1130. As shown in the *bottom* photo, of mortarless masonry, the Bonitans were master builders.

Anasazi include the Pueblo Indians, among whom are the Hopi, Zuni, and Pueblo Indians of the Rio Grande Valley in New Mexico.

People of the Mogollon culture, whose ancestors were the mountain-dwelling Cochise, occupied a region from central Arizona and New Mexico southward. By 3,000 years ago they were skilled farmers, having learned to grow maize and grind it into flour. They also gathered many wild foods including pine nuts, lily bulbs, walnuts, and acorns. They hunted deer, turkeys, bison, and muskrats, for example.

Mogollon villages of the early period consisted of pit houses. These were dome-shaped structures made of sticks, grass, and mud supported by a central pole and curved supporting ribs of wood, all resting in a pit dug knee-deep into the ground. Later, the huts became rectangular with corner posts replacing the central post. Also, pueblo-style houses

Described as the "gem of Anasazi cliff dwellings," Cliff Palace at Mesa Verde, Colorado was built around A.D. 1100 and abandoned about 1275. The apartment complex had more than 200 rooms.

built aboveground began to appear. This change in house style took place during the 800s.

The Mogollon culture is best known for its pottery, the most highly stylized and finest in the New World. They decorated their bowls, mugs, and other pottery with geometric and animal designs, including bats, frogs, turtles, and insects. Their vessels also were made to show many human activities and modes of dress. About 1100 the Mogollon culture went into decline and was snuffed out by 1250. Drought conditions may have caused their decline and they may have been absorbed by the Anasazi and helped give rise to the modern Pueblos. The only Mogollon sites that survived were a few in northern Mexico, the largest of which was Casas Grandes, a city of commerce with apartment houses and huge warehouses containing copper, seashells, and other items. Then these few remaining Mogollon centers disappeared in the 1400s.

Indians of the Salado culture settled in the region of the Gila and Salt river valleys in Arizona around 1300. Like the Mogollon, they excelled in pottery making, specializing in black-on-white designs.

The Hohokam people—Cochise desert-dwellers—made their home in the desert region of south-central Arizona, the best-known site being Snaketown. These people might also be called the "canal people." The key to their survival was the construction of hundreds of miles of canals to channel water to their desert environment. Early Hohokam settlers dug a 3-mile (5-km)-long canal to the Gila River. Snaketown was a trade center where its early merchants were middlemen trading marine shells from California, turquoise from California and New Mexico, copper and rubber from Mexico, and other raw materials and finished products including woven cotton cloth and painted pottery. Among their skills as craftsmen was the acid etching of seashells, a technique not to be developed by Europeans until centuries later.

Ancestors of the Hohokam may have moved up from Mexico sometime between 300 B.C. and A.D. 300, or the

Casa Grande, near Phoenix, Arizona, is a castlelike building three stories high, built by the Hohokam indians sometime after the year 1100. Today its remains are protected from the elements by a huge roof supported on posts.

Hohokam culture may have evolved from a people already settled in the area, the desert-dwelling Cochise. In the 1100s the Hohokam changed architectural styles from that of pit houses to houses built above ground. One of their most impressive structures is a castlelike building three stories high known as Casa Grande, south of Phoenix. Just before Columbus's voyage to America the Hohokam culture declined and died and nobody knows why. By the 1500s the eastern region of their range was occupied by Pima Indians while Papago Indians lived in the western range.

By the time these three main cultures were in decline, or had all but disappeared, other groups had drifted down from the Canadian west and north and taken up life in the Southwest. These late arrivals were the Apacheans, who included the various Apaches and Navajo and who spoke languages of the Athapaskan language group. These newcomers depended less on farming and more on a hunter-gatherer way of life. They were not the best of neighbors with the Pueblo groups in the area. Sometimes they were traders, but more often raiders.

# 10

# Indians of the Northwest Coast and Plains

Harpoons found along with sea mammal and fish remains show that Paleo-Indians had made the Northwest coast their home as early as 9,000 years ago. What happened to these early arrivals is hard to say. But more recent arrivals came to the region just ahead of the Eskimos and left many traces of how they lived. Over the centuries these people evolved cultures with names including the Nootka, Haida, Coola, Tlingit, Chinook, and others. Their languages fall into at least four language groups—Athapaskan, Wakashan, Penutian, and Salishan.

The rugged mountainous region of the Pacific Northwest tended to isolate these Indian groups and so preserve their many distinct languages. Nevertheless, the northwest groups carried on trade with each other and with the Inuits and Aleuts to the north. They traded such items as fish oil, edible roots, furs, walrus teeth, shells, baskets, and other crafts products. Indian groups of the Southwest, even though not isolated and who carried on a free-flowing cultural interchange, also preserved their individual languages—at least seven that belong to at least four language families.

Most of the groups were warlike. Their weapons included bows and arrows, short spears used as bayonets, slings, clubs, and daggers. They often made slaves of their prisoners and more often than not a slave's life was a miserable one. Slaves often were killed when their master died so that they might accompany and serve their master in the spirit world. They were sometimes deliberately crushed to death beneath massive house posts. And other times the Kwakiutl tribe, for instance, killed slaves on the beach so that their bodies could be used as log rollers to bring ashore a visiting chief's canoe. If a chief owned many slaves, he enjoyed high status among other tribes. Status among individuals of several Indian groups sometimes included how many tattoos a person had on the body.

The lush forests provided a variety of trees which were

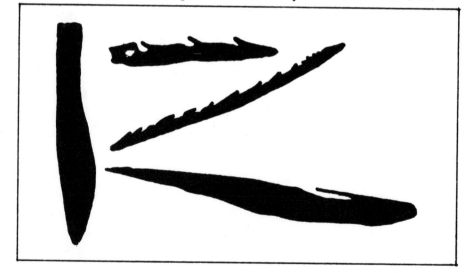

Weapons for use on land and at sea used by Paleo-Indians of the northwest coast included barbed harpoon heads (top); bone daggers used as a hand weapon or attached to a shaft (left); bone fish spears (center); and "bayonet" points of bone.

used to make storage houses of cedar planks, carved bowls and dishes, and logs for multifamily dwellings. Some of the log buildings had elaborately carved entrance pillars, which evolved into storytelling totem poles. A number of coastal groups, including the Haida, excelled at making canoes.

About 500 years ago a major mud slide buried beneath 10 feet (3 m) of clay the whale fishing village of Ozette on Washington's Olympic Peninsula. Although demolished as a living place, the village was remarkably well preserved over the centuries. Archaeologists have dug up more than 50,000 artifacts, most in excellent condition and beyond value in showing how the people of this period lived.

Spring and summer for many northwest coast groups were spent camping by the rivers where there was always a good supply of salmon. In the fall the groups returned to their villages where they passed the winter, a typical village having

Basketry hats were common among the northwest coast Indians. *At center,* one of a Kwakiutl type with painted design; *left,* a Nootkan chief's hat with a woven design; *right,* a Haida hat with the design painted.

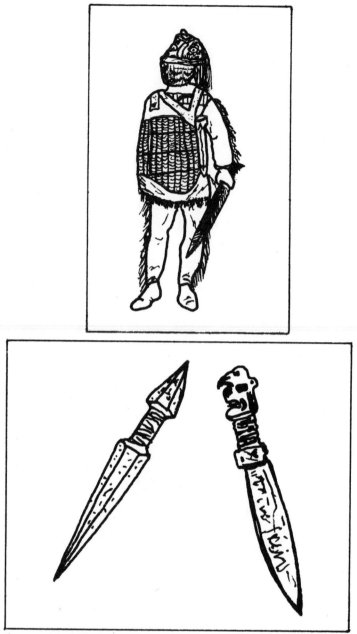

Northwest coast Indians known as the Tlingit designed sophisticated armor and arms for battle with neighboring groups. The helmet and visor were of wood while slats of wood tied together protected the body. Fighting knives, about 2 feet (0.6 meters) long, included a double-pointed iron one and a single-pointed one with a decorated haft about 18 inches (0.45 meters) long.

about 1,000 people. This was the time for an elaborate ceremony called a potlatch. It brought together the various groups making up a single tribe, or it might include groups from other communities. The purpose of a potlatch was for the host group to announce to one and all and formalize the newly given title or social status of an individual—appointment of a new chief, admission into a secret society, or the like. The guest groups served as witnesses and then were showered with fine gifts and an elaborate feast. A canoe filled with delicate salmon roe or specially prepared wild berries might be offered.

The Pacific northwest coast Indians had a rich cultural tradition and were among the last to be reached by the white man. When the meeting finally did take place on a large scale in the late 1700s, the outcome was a familiar one—widespread death and destruction. European and American traders, hungry for highly valued sea-otter pelts, in only a few years drastically reduced the sea-otter population along the coast. In exchange for the valuable pelts they gave the Indians guns, rum, cheap colored beads, and iron blades that could be used in warfare. They also introduced widespread disease among the Indians. That, combined with an increase in deadly weapons that were used in warfare among the Indian tribes, rapidly and effectively wiped out many groups and all but snuffed out others. Even so, the present-day Indians of the Pacific northwest coast have survived and maintained their cultural traditions better than most.

### The Plains Indians

The enormous region of the American plains stretches northward from Texas to Canada and lies along an east-west path from the Mississippi River to the Rocky Mountains. This sprawling region, with its herds of millions of bison, became the home for many Indian groups. They came out of the north from Canada and Alaska, from the west and southwest, and from the east. Collectively, they are called the Plains Indians.

The environment of this broad region varies with its geography. There are mountains, flatlands, stream valleys, and meadows "as far as the eye can see and thought can travel," according to one explorer. Some areas are moist, others dry, and there are sprawling grasslands. As the land varied so did the Indian cultures who made it their home.

Many groups have roamed the plains continuously for the past 10,000 years or more. Archaeologists use the term Paleo-Indians to describe the early Americans up to about 5000 B.C. Groups who came later are described as belonging to the Archaic Period. The year A.D. 950 or so marks the end of the Archaic and the beginning of the Plains Village Period. Like the Paleo-Indians before them, Indian bands of the Archaic also were hunter-gatherers, following the bison herds and other game. Until fairly recent times, the Plains Indians stampeded bison herds over cliffs in great mass killings. As the Aleuts used practically every part of a killed whale, so the Plains Indians used just about every part of a bison: They ate its meat, made tools and weapons of its bones, blankets and clothing from its hide and hair, and they used its dung (buffalo chips) as fuel. They supplemented their diet of meat with berries, fruits, and edible roots. A weapon of war and tool for hunting, the bow and arrow probably was introduced to the Plains Indians by warlike groups who moved down from the Northwest.

While Indians of the western plains were wanderers and lived in temporary shelters, such as tepees, those of the eastern plains were more settled, living in permanent villages. The Mandans, for instance, built huge earth lodges supported by thick beams and covered with sod. Several families would have shared certain areas of a lodge and also had private family quarters. Some of the community buildings were up to 60 feet (18 m) across. Permanent villages meant farming as a chief source of food. The plains villagers grew maize, beans, squash, and other foods which they dried and stored in special pits in their houses.

By the year A.D. 200 wide-ranging trade routes linked the many and scattered Indian groups of the plains, the East, Southeast, and as far west as Texas. Obsidian for knife blades and projectile points came from what today is Yellowstone National Park. Copper came from the northern Great Lakes, sheets of mica from the southern Appalachians, and shells from the Gulf Coast. Extensive trade meant frequent contact with other cultures, and frequent contacts led to a blending of cultures into interaction spheres. But cultural blending did not always mean a blending of languages. Although culturally linked, the Mandans and Arikara groups, for example, kept their distinct languages as did Indian groups of the Southwest.

By the time the American settlers from Europe arrived and began to push westward, there were hundreds of tribes spanning the plains, the names of some today representing our states—the Kansa, Omaha, Iowa, Missouri—and there were the Mandans, Hidatsa, Ponca, Osage, Wichita, Apache, and Kiowa. As had happened elsewhere, contact with the white man brought disease against which the Indians had no natural defenses. As the white man also pushed them off their land and out of their villages, the Indians' numbers decreased and their cultures decayed.

# 11

# *Indians of the Southeast and Northeast*

As you found in an earlier chapter, the oldest known Paleo-Indian site in the southeast is one at Little Salt Spring, Florida, dated as 12,000 years old. These groups used Clovis-style projectile points to hunt bison, giant ground sloths, and mastodons. Some 2,000 years later they had learned to supplement their diet with many kinds of edible plants, but they were not farmers. They still were hunter-gatherers. Food abounded for those who knew how to get it—deer, rabbits, squirrels, fish, turtles, oysters, and mussels, and seasonal plants including fruits, berries, and nuts.

A remarkable Southeast Paleo-Indian find was made at the Windover site near the present Disney World and Kennedy Space Center in Florida in 1984 by Florida State University archaeologists. So far, more than 100 burials dating from 7,000 to 8,000 years ago have been found. The burials were made in a 1-foot (0.3-m)-deep peat bog. Each body was carefully wrapped in cloth, grass mats, and covered with peat and wood. Peat is an organically rich substance made up largely of decayed vegetable matter and is a remark-

95

able preservative. The remains of these Paleo-Indians are so well preserved that biologists probably will be able to tell what kinds of diseases these ancient people had. The skill with which some of their artifacts were fashioned, and the fineness of the woven cloth preserved along with the skeletons, surprised scientists working at the site.

True farming reached the southeast by about 6,000 years ago and local populations grew rapidly with this new and dependable food source to support them. And storable food meant a need for pottery. By the late 1400s the population of the southeast may have reached 250,000 or so. Burial mounds began to appear among many North American Indian cultures about 3,000 years ago, such as the great mound on the Adena estate near Chillicothe, Ohio, built to honor the dead. The Indians of the southeast were the true Mound Builders. They built mounds by the thousands, among the earliest being mounds at Poverty Point, Louisiana, some 3,500 years old. In addition to burial mounds, there were ceremonial mounds and mounds for defense. Near Cincinnati, Ohio, is one of the most pictorial mounds. It is a quarter mile (0.4 km) long and in the shape of a serpent about to swallow an object shaped like an egg. Some mounds, such as the 70-foot (21-m)-high Grave Creek Mound in downtown Moundsville, West Virginia, were enormous.

### The Mound Builders
There were three major mound-building groups—the Adena, the Hopewell, and the Mississippians. The Adena culture dominated the Ohio Valley region for some 700 years from 500 B.C. to A.D. 200. Their chief influence lay in their burial customs. They placed their dead in pits or log tombs, then after several years burned the structure and covered it over

with sod. Over a period of 100 years or so new pits would be dug in the old mounds and so the mounds grew larger and higher. Eventually mounds joined other mounds until the structures became huge, some being enclosed by "sacred circles" of earth. There may be as many as 500 mound sites in Adena territory, which spread to Indiana, Kentucky, New York, Delaware, and Maryland.

Before the year 200 the Adena culture faded out and was replaced by the Hopewell culture. This new burial-mound cult simply expanded on Adena practices, making everything bigger and better. Emphasis was on a grander style of living—more trade, including more luxury items, and bigger, higher, and

The great Mound at Marietta, Ohio, was one constructed by Indians of the Hopewell culture. Many such mounds were burial mounds and were the scenes of elaborate burial practices to honor the dead.

more elaborate burial mounds and burial ceremonies. Imagine the extravagance of completely covering a dead person with pearls, then covering the corpse with hard-won copper, and finally surrounding it with fine pottery and sculpture.

Some Hopewell earthworks took the shape of enormous circles, squares, and eight-sided figures a quarter of a mile (0.4 km) across and containing up to thirty or so burial mounds. One of the most impressive is the Newark, Ohio, center which covers a 4-square-mile (10-sq-km) area. Why they built these enormous earthworks remains a mystery. Hopewell centers, which started in the Ohio Valley by the year 350, covered a broad belt from Louisiana north to the Great Lakes. But the culture waned in the 300s and 400s. Burial mounds became simpler and there were fewer goods reflecting Hopewell high fashion and luxury. Possibly the interaction sphere with other cultures weakened, but no one knows why the Hopewell culture gradually slipped into oblivion.

As the Adena culture gave way to the Hopewell, by the early 800s the Hopewell was replaced by the Mississippian. By this time farming was widely practiced in the Ohio Valley and eastward, and widespread use of the bow and arrow increased conflicts among certain tribes. By this time American Indian cultures were reaching the stage of development in which the European settlers found them. When the sprawling Mississippian culture peaked between 1200 and 1500, there were several thousand sites and hundreds of villages and large towns. Social rank and status had become extremely important among the widespread Mississippian groups, as it had among the Indians of the Northwest.

Near East St. Louis, Illinois, was one of the largest Mississippian towns, Cahokia. It covered some 6 square miles (16 sq km), had more than 100 mounds and a population of at least 10,000. During its peak it had at least 10 satellite villages, about 50 farming centers, plus hunting and fishing camps. In all, they sprawled over an area of 125 square miles (324 sq km).

At the center of the main town was a gigantic structure called Monks Mound built over a 300-year period. It was completed about the year 1250, a time when the Aztecs of Mesoamerica were establishing their civilization. Monks Mound was 100 feet (30.5 m) high and built with four terraces, which made it the largest man-made structure in the New World. The 22 million cubic feet (623,000 cu m) of earth making the mound was carried in baskets by thousands of workers and without the aid of horses or other work animals. America's post–Ice Age horses had become extinct and horses were not to graze over the American plains again until they were brought by the Spanish in the 1500s. Atop the mound was a 104-foot (2-m)-long building, probably a combination temple and living quarters for the town's chief. Below was a 40-acre (16-ha) square, numerous dwelling huts, and lesser mounds, all enclosed by a high wood stockade fence.

To the east of the plaza was a structure similar to England's Stonehenge. Called Woodhenge, because of its construction of wooden posts, it may have been an astronomical observatory used to pinpoint the arrival of the various seasons and signal the time for planting and harvest.

Other important Mississippian centers included Moundville, Etowah, and Spiro. Located near Tuscaloosa, Alabama, Moundville was second in importance to Cahokia. Twenty platform mounds, each with a temple-residence on top, cover an area of some 300 acres (121.4 ha). The rulers of Moundville also ruled over groups of the surrounding countryside, the total population numbering 10,000 individuals.

## Drugs and Religious Rites

While Indian groups in Mesoamerica and South America

99

were worshiping gods of lightning or storm, or sun gods and moon gods, their neighbors to the north were carrying out elaborate burial ceremonies and worshiping gods of their making, based on a combination of fear and respect for forces of the environment.

Many of the religious rites and ceremonies, and the chants and hypnotic states that were an essential part of them, depended on the use of drugs that put the high priests and worshipers alike into a state of ecstasy, or overpowering emotion and frenzy. This seems to have been true of many of the North American Indian cultures, as it was true of the Peruvian culture of Chavín described earlier when worshipers took the mind-warping plant drug mescaline. In a book he wrote around 1620, the Spaniard Ruiz de Alarcón described the widespread habit of Mexico's Aztec-speaking people taking the hallucinogenic seeds of the morning glory plant.

It is from Texas that the earliest North American evidence of the use of mind-warping plant drugs comes. It is in the form of the "mescal bean," found in a cave called Bonfire Shelter and dated at about 10,000 years old. These drug-containing "beans" are the hallucinogenic seeds of a flowering bush (*Sophora secundiflora*) and were widely planted, used, and commonly traded among North American Indian tribes until the late 1800s. So were many other drug-containing plants used to bring on trances and communication with spirits and other supernatural forces during initiation rites and religious ceremonies. Jimsonweed was another such plant used, for example, by Indians of Virginia. The Indians believed that gods were present in such plants and that to take the plant drugs was to become one with the gods. The Aztecs, for instance, called their sacred mushrooms "god's flesh."

Perhaps as many as 100 species of plant drugs were known and used by the North American Indians for use in their religious practices. To take such a drug meant your personal passage into the supernatural world. Some anthropologists suspect that the Paleo-Indian practice of taking drug-containing plants, for whatever reasons, started thousands of years earlier in Asia. The first arrivals across Beringia may have brought the practice with them and wherever they settled searched for drug-containing plants. So the reliance on drugs for religious and other purposes of the Indians of both North and South America probably was part of the cultural baggage of those first immigrants from Asia, and many of those who followed.

For some reason the impressive mound culture of the Mississippian began to decline around 1400, as had the Hopewell and Adena earlier. In some cases, fortresses replaced the ceremonial mounds. Against what enemies these fortresses were built remains an archaeological puzzle, as does the gradual abandonment of the large towns and the return of the people to simpler and less comfortable ways of life. As one observer has put it, "the mound-builders took their secrets with them to the grave."

### Indians of the Northeast

Paleo-Indians were established in the northeastern United States and Canada at least 12,000 years ago and 21,000 years ago in Pennsylvania's Meadowcroft Rockshelter. Seven thousand years ago Paleo-Indians of Labrador buried their dead in mounds of rock and earth and provided them with harpoon points, bone pendants, and other items to accompany them after death. A 4,000-year-old burial site in Port au Choix in western Newfoundland contains many grave goods that reveal the religious and magical beliefs of those seagoing people.

Until the dramatic spread of the Hopewell culture sometime around the year 300, Indians of the Northeast had pretty much followed the living patterns of their ancestors in the region, that of hunting, fishing, and gathering edible plants. As with the Indians of the northwest coast, those of the northeast coast also found a rich resource in the sea—mussels and clams, crabs, lobsters, sea bass, and numerous birds and mammals. Among the tribes in the areas of what is now New England were the Micmac, Abnaki, and Narragansett, for example. All spoke languages of the eastern Algonquian family of languages. They lived in small villages in wigwams, domed structures covered with animal skins and bark supported by small, young trees.

To the west and south were other tribes in Canada and south into New York State. New York's tribes made up five "nations" together known as the Iroquois. The tribes of these nations were the Cayuga, Seneca, Onondaga, Mohawk, and Oneida. They all spoke languages of the Iroquoian family of languages. The dwellings and settlements of the Iroquois were larger than those of the tribes to the north and east. Instead of wigwams, they lived in clusters of large (up to 100- to 300-foot [30- to 91-m]-long) houses of logs enclosed within a protective stockade. The population of such a community may have numbered a few hundred. Without access to the rich food source of the sea, the Iroquois depended on farming more than the Algonquians did.

Around the Great Lakes and south into West Virginia were the tribes Miami, Kickapoo, Winnebago, and Shawnee, among others. They were less settled than the Iroquois, practicing farming on only a limited scale and depending largely on a hunting-gathering existence. These people's dependency on maize as a major food crop meant that they had to move their villages on a fairly regular basis, since maize quickly drains the land of nutrients. Because these tribes of the Northeast were frequently fighting and raiding each other, trade among them posed certain danger. The Iroquois were especially warlike, attacking neighboring Iroquoian groups and groups of the Algonquian tribes. It is not clear whether they carried out their raids to expand their territories and so acquire more land for farming, or for some other reason.

By about 1500 Iroquois wars among the five tribes had become so common that the tribal chiefs met and called a truce. The resulting union of tribes gave them much needed strength against the European settlers, but by the late 1700s the size of the tribes had been greatly reduced by superior weapons of the Europeans. Also, diseases brought by the Europeans killed the Indians by the thousands. In many cases those who were not killed in battle or by disease were driven off their land.

The defeat of the Native Americans was bound to come in time, but it did not have to come so soon and perhaps so thoroughly. Had the Indians been as well organized as the European settlers, the Indians could have held them off. Eventually the sheer numbers of Europeans, buttressed with a rapidly growing technology, made the Indians' cause a hopeless one. As a group, the American Indians preferred their own ways and the ways of their ancestors to the ways of the Europeans. The change they would have to undergo in order to be absorbed into the European cultural pool was to them overwhelming and impossible. The rule then, as it is today, is that cultures evolve. When one culture meets in head-on conflict with the culture of another people, usually the weaker one is overwhelmed and goes into decline. That is a lesson of history and has occurred tens of thousands of times since there have been human beings on this planet.

# A SELECTION OF NORTH AMERICAN INDIAN RUINS

There are many Paleo-Indian, and later, archaeological Indian sites across the United States, thousands of them. They range from simple campsites to burial mounds to the cliff dwellings of the Southwest. To find out about these prehistoric American remains in your area, write to the park division in your state capital. And don't overlook museums that have collections of Paleo-Indian artifacts on display. Among such museums are these: Heard Museum, Phoenix, Arizona; Museum of Northern Arizona, Flagstaff; University of Colorado Museum, Boulder; Peabody Museum of Archaeology and Ethnology, Cambridge, Massachusetts; Ohio State Museum, Columbus; American Museum of Natural History, and Museum of the American Indian, New York City; U.S. National Museum, Washington, D.C.; San Francisco, Los Angeles, and Santa Barbara, California, museums also have Paleo-Indian artifacts, as do museums in Denver, Colorado; Salt Lake City, Utah; and Albuquerque, New Mexico. The most complete and up-to-date book about archaeological sites and museums in the United States and Canada is *America's Ancient Treasures,* third edition, by Franklin Folsom and Mary Elting Folsom (Albuquerque: University of New Mexico Press, 1983). Following is a brief selection of well-preserved sites of early American Indians:

**Aztec Ruins National Monument:** Located in northwestern New Mexico, just outside the town of Aztec, the site covers an area of some 25 acres (10 ha). Begun around A.D. 1100, the now crumbled ruins once stood three stories high. The houses were made of hand-cut sandstone blocks supported by timbered roofs. The main ruin at Aztec is an apartment building with 500 rooms occupied by about 1,000 people. This pueblo was occupied for about 200 years by two groups—the Chaco and the Mesa Verde. Headquarters are at the Aztec Monument, Aztec, New Mexico.

**Bandelier National Monument:** This site is in north-central New Mexico's Pajarito Plateau and covers an area of 42 square miles (110 sq km) of canyons and ridges. Built around 1200 and occupied until about 1600, 2 miles (3 km) of the north wall of the Frijoles Canyon was gouged out with stone tools to make cave dwellings. Masonry buildings from one to three stories high were then built in front of the caves. The remains of these buildings are the chief feature of Bandelier. Although Frijoles Canyon can be reached by road, other areas can be reached only by trail.

**Canyon De Chelly National Monument:** Located in the middle of the Navajo Indian Reservation, Arizona, the site covers 131 square miles (339 sq km). It is the largest of our archaeological monuments and contains 400 or more Paleo-Indian cliff dwellings, the first of which were built around the year 1066. In red sandstone cliffs rising to 800 feet (244 m) above the canyon floor are carved doorways to more than 175 rooms and ceremonial chambers called kivas in one dwelling called White House. Mummy Cave, another part of the complex, seems to be the oldest continuously occupied site in North America.

**Casa Grande National Monument:** This small site is less than 1 square mile (3 sq km), located in the Gila River Valley of south-central Arizona. The mud-stone buildings were erected in the early 1300s and were occupied for about 150 years. This was the region of first the Hohokam and then Pueblo Indians known as Salados who excelled at architecture and built Casa Grande village. The Pima Indian reservation is 5 miles (8 km) northwest of Casa Grande. Casa Grande is the only remaining building of the former village. It is a four-story, eleven-room structure some 40 by 60 feet (12 by 18 m). Poles of juniper, pine, and oak were floated downriver from mountains 50 miles (80 km) away. Rattlesnakes, Gila monsters, tarantulas, and scorpions are the most frequent visitors to the site.

**Chaco Canyon National Monument:** In Bloomfield, New Mexico, this spectacular prehistoric site covers 33 square miles (86 sq km) and contains eighteen major ruins built by Paleo-Indians from about A.D. 920 to 1130. The most impressive is Pueblo Bonita ("Beautiful City"). One of the largest apartment houses in the world up to 1887, the huge D-shaped remains cover 3 acres (1 ha), was about 5 stories high, and had 800 rooms and 32 circular kivas. It could house up to 1,200 people. Of higher quality than any other pueblo dwelling, each stone of Pueblo Bonito was cut to fit in place. Associated with the site are fine pottery remains and turquoise jewelry; both evidence of contact with Mesoamerican cultures farther to the south.

**Effigy Mounds National Monument:** Three miles north of Marquette, Iowa, overlooking the Mississippi River. Many of the mounds in this group covering about 2 square miles (5 sq km) are shaped like birds and other animals and are up to 70 feet (21 m) wide, 140 feet (43 m) long, and 4 feet (1 m) high. The Effigy Mound builders seem to have been active from about A.D. 900 to the time of Columbus's voyage. The mounds were used for burials and are associated with numerous artifacts—pottery, bone, stone, and metal tools.

**Gila Cliff Dwellings National Monument:** 30 miles (50 km) from Silver City, New Mexico, in a canyon among the Mogollon Mountains. Covering 160 acres (65 ha) it has five caves and associated prehistoric dwellings well preserved. One cave has several small rooms. Another is high up the cliff and can be reached only by ladder.

**Grand Canyon National Park:** In Arizona, accessible from the North Rim or the South Rim. Of many prehistoric Indian sites in and near the canyon's rim, only three have been excavated. Many remain to be excavated, among them some ancient dwellings in the canyon's walls. Those sites open to the public include Tusayan Ruin, a village located on the South Rim at the Wayside Museum of Archaeology. Cape Royal Ruin, located on the North Rim, is another, as is Bright Angel Pueblo on the canyon bottom. Indians took up life in the canyon some 3,000 to 4,000 years ago.

**Hovenweep National Monument:** Forty miles (64 km) west of Cortez, Colorado, on the Utah-Colorado border, covering less than a half square mile (1 sq km) are unusual towers built by Pueblo Indians in the 1100s. Some of the stone towers are rectangular, others circular, and some D-shaped. All overlook the canyon. Some still stand their original three stories high and are expertly made, with stonework of the same quality of the stone walls at nearby Mesa Verde. The towers seem to have been permanent dwellings used as fortresses by farmers who then worked the surrounding rich farmlands. When drought dried up the farmlands these Indians seem to have moved southward in search of fertile land.

**Mesa Verde National Park:** Located in southwestern Colorado, has more ancient villages and dwellings than any other site in the United States. It had a long history of occupation from A.D. 1 to about 1300. Only a few of the many dwellings have been studied and the area is known as an "archaeologist's paradise." There are pit houses grouped in villages and hundreds of pueblo ruins on the canyon floor and mesa top. Among them is Far View House once containing about 50 rooms. Cliff Palace contains about 200 dwellings. Spruce Tree House is the second largest with 114 dwellings. The great drought of 1276–99 is thought to have destroyed this civilization.

**Montezuma Castle National Monument:** One of the best preserved cliff dwellings in North America. Located in central

Arizona, the pueblo settlement is built into a limestone cliff overlooking Beaver Creek Valley. One hundred feet (31 m) high, the cliff has dwellings build into a large recess protected by an overhang on the ledge. The castle is the centerpiece. Made of limestone blocks held together with mortar, it is 40 feet high (12 m) and has 20 rooms. Around the year 700 Indians settled in this area, at which time they found fertile fields. Four hundred years later other Indian groups from the north also settled in the area. In the late 1300s the area seems to have been struck by drought and was abandoned.

**Mound City Group National Monument:** Four miles (6 km) from Chillicothe, Ohio. This thousand-year-old site covers 57 acres (23 ha) and contains 24 burial mounds in a 13-acre (5-ha) enclosure bounded by an earth wall. People of the Hopewell culture used Mound City as a ceremonial site for the burial of their dead.

**Navajo National Monument:** Located within the Navajo Indian Reservation in northeastern Arizona. Covering 360 acres (146 ha) the monument contains the most spectacular prehistoric cave villages in the state. There are three settlements—Betatakin, Keet Seel, and Inscription House. Betatakin, the largest, is truly impressive. Seven hundred years old, its buildings occupy an enormous natural cave cut into the red sandstone cliffs of a 500-foot (152-m) -deep forested canyon. Above the cave is a huge arch that reaches a height of 236 feet (72 m). There are more than fifty dwellings making up the village which is reached over a mile and a half (2 km) of steep switchback trails. The other two villages have their own special attractions.

**Old Kasaan National Monument:** Marks the ruins of a Haida Indian village in southeastern Alaska on the east shore of Prince of Wales Island. There is little left on the site except for disintegrating monuments, totem poles, and grave houses.

The Haidas abandoned the village when white men offered them employment in fish canneries. Vandals then ransacked the old village and carted off what artifacts were worth taking for sale.

**Ocmulgee National Monument:** In Macon, Georgia, about 1 square mile (3 sq km) in area. This monument has nine prehistoric mounds built by the Macon Plateau people around 1350. One of these ceremonial mounds used to honor the dead is 40 feet (12 m) high and 300 feet (91 m) across its base. There also is a ceremonial earth lodge 42 feet (13 m) wide and with a clay platform shaped like the head of an eagle. The remains of a village and an ancient cornfield also are part of the monument.

**Petrified Forest National Park:** Located east of Holbrook, Arizona, this site has rock carvings (petroglyphs) and a number of prehistoric ruins. The site was occupied around A.D. 500 and remained occupied for almost 1,000 years. The first dwellings were pit houses, which were followed by dwellings of stone. Restoration has begun on Agate House, a ruin near the Rainbow Forest entrance to the park. Another ruin is the Puerco Indian Ruins, a pueblo made up of some 150 rooms.

**Serpent Mound State Park:** Between Hillsboro and Portsmouth, Ohio. Some find this the most spectacular mound in the United States. A masterpiece in earth sculpture, it forms more than 1,000 feet (305 m) of a sinuous serpent poised along a ridge of land. The enormous head rests on a cliff overlooking a small river. In the center of the head, an oval embankment, are the stone remains of an ancient altar or fireplace around which several people could witness whatever rites were performed there.

**Tonto National Monument:** Two well-preserved cave dwellings occupying an area of one and a half square miles (4 sq km) in Cholla Canyon, southern Arizona. Unfortunately, vandals toppled some of the walls of the site, but much remains. There is a lower and upper site. The lower one is a cave 85 feet (6 m) wide and 40 feet (12 m) deep at the base of a cliff and has seventeen rooms at ground level and five rooms on a second level. The upper one, better preserved, has thirty-two rooms below and fourteen above. Tonto construction was not as good as those of other cliff-dwelling Indians, which does not distract from its historical importance. Their pottery, however, was of superior quality. "Tonto," by the way, is a Spanish word for "fool." The Tonto dwellings were built around 1350, a time when other Indian cultures were abandoning their settlements because of drought.

**Tuzigoot National Monument:** In central Arizona, a large ruin called Tuzigoot tops a 120-foot (37-m)-high hill looking over the Verde River valley. An example of a hilltop village pueblo, its walls of stone are held together with mortar. Because tons of sand buried the village, looters and vandals were not able to destroy it. The "citadel of the pueblo" stands on top of the hill and contains 110 rooms. It is 500 feet (152 m) long and about 100 feet (31 m) wide. Access to the rooms was by ladders down through the roof, not through doors, for protection. The early pueblo-builders in this area came around the year 1000. One of their buildings evolved into the Tuzigoot structure. By the early 1300s many other pueblo dwellings were constructed in the region. The end of the Tuzigoot settlement may have been caused by poor sanitation, disease, and overpopulation. These conditions continue to plague many parts of the world today.

**Walnut Canyon National Monument:** In central Arizona near Flagstaff, this 3-mile (5-km)-long area has about 200 small cliff dwellings along the canyon walls. It was occupied around A.D. 1100 by farming Indians who remained in the area for nearly 200 years. A pit house is on view for visitors. Before the site was protected, vandals pushed over the stone walls and took many valuable artifacts. If you visit the site, be sure to see Sunset Crater, a volcano that erupted in A.D. 1065.

**Wupatki National Monument:** In north-central Arizona, this reservation extends over 56 square miles (145 sq km) and has many well-preserved ruins. A volcanic eruption in A.D. 1065 covered an 800-square-mile (2,070-sq-km) area with volcanic cinder that subsequently enabled the soil to retain water. This fact attracted nearby Indian farmers, among them the Mogollon, Anasazi, and Hohokam, who formed a cultural alliance with the Sinagua, who had inhabited the area before the volcano erupted. The area was thriving around A.D. 1100 but by 100 years later the many cornfields dried up due to a combination of intensive farming and the water-retaining cinder mulch being blown away. The people left the area, their descendants now living about 50 miles (80 km) away in Hopi villages.

**Yucca House National Monument:** In southwestern Colorado, this site is a prehistoric Indian village that covers 10 acres (4 ha) on the eastern slope of Sleeping Ute Mountain. The site has not been excavated and is nearly covered by high mounds. The pueblo village was occupied from about A.D. 1000 to 1300 by Anasazi Indians. Visits to the site by the public are not encouraged until the area can be excavated by archaeologists. The site is hard to find and the unimproved roads often are impassable.

This listing of prehistoric Indian ruins is based on information contained in *Exploring Our Prehistoric Indian Ruins,* by Devereux Butcher and published by the National Parks Association, Washington, D.C.

# Glossary

**Aleut**—The various peoples from Asia, and offshoots of the Inuit (Eskimos), who settled in the Aleutian Islands near Alaska about 3,000 years ago.

**alluvial fan**—A fan-shaped deposit of rocks, gravel, sand, and other materials formed by a stream the water of which suddenly slows so that the gravels and other materials it carries quickly settle to the bottom.

**anthropology**—The "study of man," including social organization, customs and beliefs, language, and physical aspects of people living today and who lived long ago.

**archaeology**—The study of the history and cultures of peoples who lived in the past by discovering and interpreting the material remains they left behind.

**Archaic Period**—That period in the American West after 5000 B.C. which includes Indian cultures that came after the Paleo-Indians. The Archaic lasted until A.D. 950, at which time the Plains Village Period began. In the eastern woodlands the Archaic Period began in 8000 B.C. with the Dalton culture.

**artifact**—Any object, including tools and weapons, made by human beings. In this book artifacts include such items as projectile points, harpoons, and arrowheads, for example.

**atlatl**—A spear-throwing stick notched at one end so that the handle end of a spear could be fitted into the notch and then flung with the action of a lever (the atlatl). The atlatl enabled a spear to be thrown with greater force and over a greater distance than by hand alone. The atlatl is used to this day by Australian aborigines who call it a woomera.

**Beringia**—A bridge of land linking Asia and Alaska, actually the floor of the Bering Sea exposed when sea level lowered during the last glacial period. Animals and people were able to cross over Beringia from Asia into the New World.

**bifacial**—Referring to projectile points that have been flaked on both surfaces to produce a highly sharpened cutting edge. Both Clovis and Folsom points were bifacial.

**chopper**—A sharpened piece of flint or other kind of stone used to cut up slaughtered animals.

**Classic Period**—That period of Mesoamerican culture dated from A.D. 300 to A.D. 900.

**climate**—A region's weather averaged over a long span of time. From the Greek word *klima,* meaning "slope" or "incline," and referring to the degree of slant of the sun's rays relative to the earth's surface.

**Clovis point**—A spear tip made by flaking obsidian, chert, or other fine-grained stones on both sides (bifacial) and finally chipping out a hollow on each side so that the point is fluted. The chipped-out hollow enabled the point to be fixed to the end of a spear shaft with a thong. Clovis points were first discovered in New Mexico and were made by people living in New Mexico between 11,000 and 11,600 years ago.

**Cro-Magnon man**—Modern man, who replaced Neanderthal man in Europe about 30,000 years ago, in Africa about 60,000 years ago, and in Southeast Asia about 40,000 years ago.

**cultural province**—The result of several small cultures blending and living as one. There were three main cultural provinces of the American Southwest: the Anasazi, the Hohokam, and the Mogollon.

**culture**—The customs, equipment, techniques, manufactures, ideas, language, and beliefs of a people, such as the Aztec, Maya, or Pueblo Indians, for example.

**early arrivalists**—The group of anthropologists who think that the Paleo-Indians came to America at least 30,000 years ago, and possibly earlier than 100,000 years ago.

**flesher**—A tool used to scrape the flesh away from the hide of a freshly killed animal. A broad bone fashioned so that it had sharp and flat "teeth" was commonly used.

**fluted**—Referring to stone projectile points, such as Clovis and Folsom, the faces of which had a long notch flaked out so that the point could be securely tied to the end of a shaft and so used as a spear tip.

**Folsom point**—A projectile point smaller and more elegant than the earlier Clovis points. Folsom points were pressure-flaked rather than being flaked by striking. The craftsman pressed a tool hard enough at a spot near the point's edge to chip off a small flake. The Folsom people improved on the Clovis point by refining it. The flutes of a Folsom point extended nearly the entire length of the point on both faces.

**genus**—A broad grouping of organisms all of which have certain characteristics in common but which belong to different species. For example, there are various species of the genus *Homo*. *Homo sapiens* means "wise man" while *Homo habilis* refers to a manlike species that lived long ago. All members of the same genus are descended from a fairly recent common ancestor.

**geofact**—Any object of stone, bone, or wood, for example, that has been worn or otherwise worked by nature so that it resembles an object (artifact) worked by the hands of human beings.

**glacier**—Any mass of moving land ice formed out of compacted snow. There are eight principal forms of glaciers.

**hunter-gatherers**—People who rely on wild game, fruits, and what other wild foods happen to be in season. A hunter-gatherer existence requires less energy than does a way of life that depends on agriculture. Many groups must have been forced into a hunter-gatherer way of life as a result of being displaced from rich environments by stronger groups and thereafter had to content themselves with marginal lands where one had to move often to make ends meet.

**ice age**—Any extended period of time during which a substantial portion of Earth's surface is covered by "permanent" ice. There have been seven known major ice ages during the past 700,000 years, with the last Ice Age reaching its peak about 18,000 years ago.

**interaction sphere**—The result of two or more cultures exchanging ideas or technology so that each culture is enriched with qualities of the others.

**interglacial period**—A period of warming between two glacial periods. Some climatologists think that we are now enjoying an interglacial period between the last glacial period which ended about 10,000 years ago and the next one.

**Inuit**—The native name for the Eskimos.

**language family**—A group of languages similar enough to each other to be considered a family but distinct enough not to be readily understood by an outsider of the same language family. The Iroquoian language family, for example, includes the individual languages of Seneca, Mohawk, and Cherokee. In a similar way French, Italian, and Spanish belong to the Romance language family.

**late arrivalists**—Those anthropologists who think that the Paleo-Indians came to America not much earlier than about 12,000 years ago.

**Mesoamerica**—Middle or Central America, including the region between the southernmost part of North America and the northernmost part of South America.

**middle arrivalists**—Those anthropologists who think that the Paleo-Indians came to America sometime between 12,000 and 30,000 years ago.

**mountain glacier**—A glacier that begins to form in the mountains, enlarges as increasing amounts of snow are compacted into it and changed to ice, and flows to lower levels, eventually sprawling over the land.

**Neanderthal man**—Large-jawed people who lived across Europe into the Near East and into central Asia. About 5 feet (2 m) tall, they were strong and had large bones. They became extinct about 35,000 years ago.

**Paleo-Indians**—Any of those groups of people who entered the Americas from Asia up to 5000 B.C. and who hunted now extinct or locally exterminated animals. Most researchers think that the Paleo-Indians crossed over to the New World over a sprawling land bridge that existed near the end of the last glacial period.

**pit house**—A dome-shaped structure made of sticks, grass, and mud supported by a central pole and curved supporting ribs of wood, all resting in a pit dug knee-deep into the ground.

**Plains Village Period**—That period following the Archaic Period and beginning about A.D. 950.

**Post-Classic Period**—That period of Mesoamerican culture dating after A.D. 900.

**postmolds**—Stains in the soil caused by the decay of wood which, on rotting, chemically discolored the soil.

**potlatch**—A cermony of the Indians of the northwest coast held when various groups making up a single tribe gathered, or it might include groups from other tribes as well. The ceremony, featuring a huge feast, formalized a newly given title or social status of an individual—appointment of a new chief, for example. The guests served as witnesses.

**Pre-Classic Period**—That period of Mesoamerican culture dating from about 1250 B.C. to A.D. 300.

**pressure flaking**—Making a projectile point by pressing a tool hard enough at a spot near the point's edge to chip off a small flake rather than by striking. By working around the edge of the point in this way, an elegant and razor-sharp cutting blade could be made. This method was typical of the Folsom point, a bifacial and fluted point which was an improvement over the Clovis point.

**pueblo**—An apartment-house village of which many were developed by American Indians of the Southwest, Pueblo Bonito, in New Mexico's Chaco Canyon, being the most famous.

**race**—Most anthropologists recognize three races of human beings—Caucasoid (light-skinned), Negroid (dark-skinned), and Mongoloid (intermediate with high cheekbones). There are five races if the Australian aborigines and American Indians are counted as separate races.

**radiocarbon dating**—Determining the age of a substance by the study of the ratio of stable "daughter" elements to their radioactive "parent" element.

**species**—All members of populations capable of interbreeding with each other. For example, since all domestic dogs are capable of interbreeding, no matter what breed they may be, they all are grouped into a single species.

118

# Further Reading

BOOKS

Bennett, Wendell C. and Bird, Junius B. *Andean Culture History,* New York: Natural History Press, 1964.

Brennan, Louis A. *Artifacts of Prehistoric America,* Harrisburg, Pa.: Stackpole, 1975.

Burland, C.A. *The Ancient Maya,* New York: John Day, 1967.

Coe, Michael D. Snow, Dean, and Benson, Elizabeth *Atlas of Ancient America,* New York: Facts on File, 1986.

Coe, Michael D. *America's First Civilization,* New York: American Heritage, 1968.

Drucker, Philip. *Indians of the Northwest Coast,* New York: Natural History Press, 1955.

Folsom, Franklin, and Folsom, Mary Elting *America's Ancient Treasures,* Albuquerque, N.M.: University of New Mexico Press, 1983.

Kopper, Philip. *The Smithsonian Book of North American Indians,* Washington, D.C.: Smithsonian Books, 1986.

Lowie, Robert H., *Indians of the Plains,* New York: Natural History Press, 1954.

Macgowan, Kennety, and Joseph A. Hester, Jr. *Early Man in the New World,* New York: Natural History Press, 1962.

McIntyre, Loren. *The Incredible Incas,* Washington, D.C.: National Geographic, 1975.

Morris, Walter F. Jr. *Living Maya,* New York: Abrams, 1987.

——, *Mysteries of the Ancient Americas,* Pleasantville, N.Y.: Reader's Digest, 1986.

Stewart, T.D., *The People of America,* New York: Scribner's, 1973.

Snell, Tee Loftin *America's Beginnings,* Washington, D.C.: National Geographic, 1974.

Stuart, George E. *Discovering Man's Past in the Americas,* Washington, D.C.: National Geographic, 1969.

Vaillant, George C. *Aztecs of Mexico,* New York: Doubleday, 1962.

Waters, Frank, *Book of the Hopi,* New York: Ballentine, 1963.

Wormington, H.M., *Ancient Man in North America,* Denver, Co.: Denver Museum of Natural History, 1957.

PERIODICALS

Adovasio J.M., and Carlisle, R.C. "Pennsylvania Pioneers," *Natural History,* December 1986, p. 20.

Bryan, A.L. "Points of Order," *Natural History,* June 1987, p. 6.

Canby, T.Y. "The Anasazi," *National Geographic,* November 1982, pp. 554-92.

Canby, Vincent. "Search for the First Americans," *National Geographic,* September 1979, pp. 330-363.

Goodman, A.H., and Armelagos, G.J. "Disease and Death at Dr. Dickson's Mounds," *Natural History,* September 1985, p. 12.

Goodwin, D.V. "Raiders of the Sacred Sites," *N.Y. Times Magazine,* December 7, 1986, p. 64.

Grayson, D.K. "Death by Natural Causes," *Natural History,* May 1987, p. 8.

Irving, W.N. "New Dates from Old Bones," *Natural History,* February 1987, p. 8.

Jimenez Moreno, W. "The Peopling of the Americas," *UNESCO Courier,* December 1983, pp. 38-9.

Lawren, B. "New World Mummies," *Omni,* January 1986, p. 20.

Lewin, R. "The First Americans Are Getting Younger," *Science,* 27 November, 1987, p. 1230.

Matheny, R.T. "El Mirador," *National Geographic,* September, 1987, pp. 317-339.

Nickell, Joe. "The Big Picture," *Scientific American,* June 1983, p. 84.

Robins, J. "Violating History," *National Parks,* July/August 1987, pp. 26-31.

Ruhlen, M. "Voices from the Past," *Natural History,* March 1987, p. 6.

Schiller, R. "The Mysteries of America's 'Ancient Ones,'" *Readers Digest,* April 1985, pp. 119-23.

Skow, J. "This Florida Spa Holds a Surprising Lode of Prehistory," *Smithsonian,* December 1986, pp. 72-8.

Stanford, D.J. "The Ginsberg Experiment," *Natural History,* September 1987, p. 10.

Zegura S.L. "Blood Test," *Natural History,* July 1987, p. 8.

A continuing source of up-to-date information on Paleo-Indians is *Mammoth Trumpet,* a newspaper-format publication. It reports current activities and publications dealing with archaeological digs that reveal information about the peopling of the Americas. It is published quarterly by the Center for the Study of Early Man, University of Maine, 495 College Ave., Orono, ME 04473.

# Index

Pre-Classic Period, 64-66
projectile points, 15
  Clovis, 31, 34-36, 39, 41, 51, 52, 95
  El Jobo, 50-51
Pueblo Indians, 81, 83, 84, 86
Pyramids, 66

**R**
radiocarbon dating, 39, 40, 46-47, 50-53, 57-59
Rasmussen, Knud, 78
religious rites, 100-102

**S**
Salishan language group, 87
San Lorenzo, Mexico, 65, 66
Santa Rosa Island, Calif., 57
Schwachheim, Carl, 32
Senecas, 61, 102
Serpent Mound State Park, 109
Shawnees, 102
Simpson, Ruth, 58-60
slavery, 88
Snaketown, Ariz., 85
Southeast Indians, 95-101
Southwest Indians, 77, 80-86
  languages of, 61-62, 93
Stalker, Archie MacS., 58
Stanford, Dennis, 15, 51, 60
Stewart, T.D., 78, 79
Stirling, Matthew, 65

**T**
Taber, Canada, 58
Taima-Taima, Venezuela, 50
Tenochtitlán, Mexico, 70
Teotihuacán, Mexico, 66
Thunderbird, Va., 49
Tierra del Fuego, 42, 43
Tlapacoya, Mexico, 52
Tlingit culture, 87, 90
Toca do Boqueirão da Pedra Furada, Brazil, 53
Toltecs, 70
Tonto National Monument, 109-10

trade, 64, 81, 87, 93, 97, 103
Tres Zapotes, Mexico, 65
Turner, Christy G., II, 28-29
Tuzigoot National Monument, 110

**V**
Vail, Maine, 40, 41
Valsequillo, Mexico, 52

**W**
Wakashan languages, 87
Walnut Canyon National Monument, 110-11
warlike tribes, 88, 102-3
Wenatchee, Wash., 37, 39
Wichitas, 93
Wilson Butte Cave, Idaho, 52
Windover, Fla., 95
Winnebagos, 102
Woodhenge, Ill., 99
Woolley, John, 57-58
Wray, Colo., 15, 16
Wupatki National Monument, 111

**Y**
Yucca House National Monument, 111

**Z**
Zapotecs, 69
Zunis, 61, 83

# About the Author

*School Library Journal* called Roy A. Gallant "one of the deans of science writers for children." He has written extensively in the field of astronomy, and *Ancient Indians: The First Americans* is his third book on archaeology.

His books for young people have received national recognition, including awards from the Thomas Alva Edison Foundation and the National Science Teachers Association. He is a recognized textbook author and consultant and is widely published in magazines such as *Science and Children*, *Omni*, and *The American Biology Teacher*.

Formerly on the faculty of the Hayden Planetarium in New York City, since 1979 Roy Gallant has been the director of the Southworth Planetarium at the University of Southern Maine. In 1987 he joined the advisory board of the Center for the Study of Early Man at the University of Maine.

When Gallant is not writing books or running planetarium shows, he usually can be found flying an airplane or taking photographs of natural history subjects.